THE GREAT
HISPANIC HERITAGE

Juan

Ponce de León

THE GREAT HISPANIC HERITAGE

Miguel de Cervantes

Cesar Chavez

Frida Kahlo

Juan Ponce de León

Diego Rivera

Pancho Villa

THE GREAT HISPANIC HERITAGE

Juan Ponce de León

Louise Chipley Slavicek

CHELSEA HOUSE
PUBLISHERS
A Haights Cross Communications Company
Philadelphia

For Krista and Nathan Slavicek

CHELSEA HOUSE PUBLISHERS
VP, New Product Development Sally Cheney
Director of Production Kim Shinners
Creative Manager Takeshi Takahashi
Manufacturing Manager Diann Grasse

Staff for JUAN PONCE DE LEÓN
Assistant Editor Kate Sullivan
Production Editor Jaimie Winkler
Photo Editor Sarah Bloom
Series & Cover Designer Terry Mallon
Layout 21st Century Publishing and Communications, Inc.

A Haights Cross Communications ◀ Company

http://www.chelseahouse.com

First Printing

1 3 5 7 9 8 6 4 2

Library of Congress Cataloging-in-Publication Data

Slavicek, Louise Chipley, 1956–
   Juan Ponce de León / Louise Chipley Slavicek.
      p. cm.—(The great Hispanic heritage)
Includes bibliographical references and index.
   ISBN 0-7910-7255-XHC   07910-7518-4PB
   1. Ponce de León, Juan, 1460?–1521—Juvenile literature. 2. Explorers—America—
Biography—Juvenile literature. 3. Explorers—Spain—Biography—Juvenile literature.
4. America—Discovery and exploration—Spanish—Juvenile literature. [1. Ponce de
León, Juan, 1460?-1521. 2. Explorers. 3. America—Discovery and exploration—
Spanish.] I. Title. II. Series.
E125.P7 S58 2003
972.9'02'092—dc21

                                                                                    2002153505

Table of Contents

The Elusive Conquistador

For many people, the name Juan Ponce de León and the fable of the fountain of youth are inextricably linked. According to the account that most of us were taught in school, the famed Spanish explorer stumbled upon Florida while on a romantic quest to find the rejuvenating fountain of Indian legends.

Yet, like just about everything else connected with Juan Ponce de León, scholars disagree regarding the mythical fountain's role in spurring the voyage that led to his discovery of Florida for Spain in 1513. Many historians believe that finding the fountain of youth was a secondary motive for Ponce at best, and that the chief incentives for his daring expedition of 1513 were similar to those of other New World conquistadors—a craving for adventure, for wealth, and for prestige. Other scholars assign more importance to the magical fountain as a motivating factor in Ponce's voyage, but argue it was the explorer's aging sponsor, Spain's King Ferdinand, and not Juan Ponce himself, who had

The story of Juan Ponce de León's search for the legendary fountain of youth is well known. Yet historians disagree on how important the legendary spring was to Ponce's journeys to the Americas. Many believe that Ponce, like other European explorers, was primarily seeking adventure, wealth, and prestige.

reason to seek the fabled spring whose waters made old men young again.

The significance of the fountain of youth in inspiring Ponce de León's voyage of discovery is only one area of contention among historians regarding the renowned explorer.

Historians have put forth widely differing opinions regarding virtually every aspect of Ponce's life and deeds from his date of birth to his parentage to exactly where he landed in Florida. Over the centuries, the nature of Ponce's moral character has also been hotly debated among scholars. Was he a heartless murderer and exploiter of the Indians as the sixteenth-century historian Bartolomé de las Casas accuses, or did Ponce treat the New World's native inhabitants with a degree of compassion and fairness remarkable for his time, as several of his other biographers claim?

A principal reason for the many scholarly disagreements regarding Ponce's background and conduct is the nature of the available sources on the *conquistador* (a leader in the Spanish conquest of the Americas, especially in the sixteenth century). Only a handful of primary sources relating to Ponce's life and career have come down to us over the years, including just two letters written by Ponce himself and some miscellaneous legal and government documents. No diaries or journals or ships' logs have survived the depredations (ravages) of time. Moreover, not a shred of archaeological evidence has been located to help pinpoint the sites of Ponce's two expeditions into Florida in 1513 and in 1521.

Because of the scarcity of original sources relating to Juan Ponce de León, his biographers have had to rely almost entirely on secondary sources published decades after the explorer's death in 1521. Chief among these secondary works are accounts by three sixteenth-century Spanish chroniclers of the New World, all of which must be used with caution: Antonio de Herrera y Tordesillas' *Historia general* (*General History*), which provides a lengthy account of the 1513 expedition to Florida but fails to offer any documentation for its sources, Gonzalo Fernández de Oviedo's *Historia general y natural de las indias* (*General and Natural History of the Indies*), which includes a brief and highly flattering account of Ponce and his New World exploits, and various writings by Bartolomé de las Casas, a passionate advocate of the Indians who detested Ponce for what Las Casas viewed as Ponce's abusive treatment of the Caribbean's native peoples, particularly on the two islands where Ponce spent most of his adult life: Hispaniola and Puerto Rico. Other more recent secondary works about Ponce include several biographies by twentieth-century Spanish and Puerto Rican historians. Just two full-length biographies of Ponce in the English language have been published: *Juan Ponce de León, King Ferdinand and the Fountain of Youth* by Anthony Devereux (1993) and *Juan Ponce de León and the Spanish Discovery of Puerto Rico and Florida* by the historical geographer Robert Fuson (2000).

What, then, are we to make of Juan Ponce de León, the man whom the historian Samuel Eliot Morison has called "the most elusive of the early conquistadors?" We will probably never know the whole truth regarding Ponce's family background, New

LAS CASAS AND THE BLACK LEGEND OF SPANISH COLONIALISM

Bartolomé de las Casas first came to the New World as a teenager in 1502. By 1514, he had become a fervent defender of the New World's native peoples against their Spanish overlords, whom he denounced as cruel and unjust. From the late sixteenth century on, Las Casas' often-exaggerated accounts of his countrymen's brutality toward the Indians were used by Spain's enemies—particularly England—as anti-Spanish propaganda, spawning the so-called "Black Legend" of Spanish colonialism. According to the legend, no colonial nation was as ruthlessly exploitative of the peoples under their rule as Spain. Today, most scholars agree that the Spanish were no crueler than other conquerors throughout the ages, and point out that it was the diseases they inadvertently brought with them from Europe, not their mistreatment of the Indians, that resulted in the high mortality rate among the New World's native peoples during the decades following Spanish settlement of the region.

Though nearly everyone recognizes Ponce de León as a bold explorer, it may surprise some to know that he was also an enterprising farmer and businessman, a resolute military commander, and the first colonial governor of Puerto Rico.

World exploits, or moral character, but what is evident, at least, is that he was an individual of many facets: an impoverished Spanish teenager who boldly determined to seek his fortune in the New World 3,000 miles away from home, an enterprising and successful farmer and businessman on the islands of Hispaniola and Puerto Rico, a resolute military commander who helped suppress two major Indian revolts against Spanish rule with ruthless efficiency, a capable administrator who served as Puerto Rico's first colonial governor, and above all, an intrepid and resourceful explorer, whose observations regarding the Atlantic current, the Gulf Stream, helped enrich his native land by providing its treasure ships with a swift route back home from the Americas, and whose discovery of Florida for his king inaugurated three centuries of Spanish hegemony in the region.

2

Youth of a Castilian Squire

Most historians believe that Juan Ponce de León was born in the village of Santervás de Campos in what is today the province of Valladolid in north central Spain. When Ponce entered the world sometime in the late fifteenth century, however, Spain as we know it today did not yet exist. Until 1516, when the nation of Spain was officially created by King Carlos I, the Iberian Peninsula was divided among a number of different kingdoms, including the narrow realm of Portugal bordering the Atlantic Ocean in the west, and three kingdoms that would eventually become the new state of Spain: Aragon, edging the Mediterranean Sea in the east, tiny Navarre to the northwest of Aragon, and Castile in the vast central portion of the peninsula. Named for the numerous castles that dotted its landscape from early medieval times, Castile was the biggest and most powerful of the Iberian kingdoms. Although largely landlocked, it was also home to Juan Ponce de León and most of the conquistadors who sailed to the New World in the late fifteenth and early sixteenth centuries.

When Juan Ponce de León was born, the country that we now know as Spain was divided into three separate Iberian kingdoms: Aragon, Navarre, and Castile. Named for the many castles that adorned its landscape, Castile was the largest and most powerful of these kingdoms. It was also home to many important sixteenth-century explorers, including Ponce de León. Some of these castles still remain, looming majestically over the Spanish landscape.

Historians generally concur regarding Ponce's place of birth, but there is less agreement regarding his date of birth. No baptismal record or other document noting Ponce's exact birth date has ever been located. This is hardly surprising since local archives in Spain were often carelessly maintained. Weather or insects seriously damaged numerous records over the centuries and some public papers vanished altogether.

For many years, historians believed that Ponce was born in 1460, the birth date provided by one of the New World's early chroniclers. Then researchers scouring Spain's archives discovered a document related to a court proceeding in Castile on September 28, 1514, in which Ponce testified that he was 40 years of age. This new piece of information indicated that Ponce was born in 1474. Yet not all scholars accepted the 1474 birth date. Some clung to the earlier date, while the prominent Spanish historian Vincente Murga Sanz further confused the issue by suggesting a third possible birth date for Ponce. In the middle of the twentieth century, while doing research on Ponce in San Juan, Puerto Rico, Murga Sanz claimed to have spotted a court document dated September 23, 1519, in which Ponce testified he was 50 years of age, thus suggesting a birth date of 1469. Since no subsequent researcher has been able to locate the 1519 court document in Puerto Rico's archives, however, Robert Fuson, Anthony Devereux, and a number of other recent scholars favor the 1474 birth date as the correct one.

Although a birth record or other contemporary document providing the names of Juan's father and mother has yet to be located, many scholars are convinced that Ponce belonged to a noble and renowned Castilian family. Fuson identifies Rodrigo Ponce de León, the Duke and Marquis of Cadiz and the most honored Castilian warrior of his day, as Juan Ponce's cousin. Juan's father was Pedro Ponce de León, Lord of Villagarcia, Fuson believes, and his paternal grandmother the aristocratic Teresa de Guzmán, La Señora de la Casa Toral (the Lady of the House of Toral).

One of the few pieces of information that has come down to us regarding Ponce's earliest years lends support to Fuson's claim that Juan was a member of the aristocratic Ponce de León-Guzmán clan. According to the sixteenth-century Spanish historians Gonzalo Fernández de Oviedo and Bartolomé de las Casas, Juan spent most of his childhood as a page and squire in the home of a distinguished Guzmán—Don (Sir) Pedro Núñez de Guzmán, Knight Commander of the Order of Calatrava. In fifteenth-century Castile, boys of aristocratic parentage were commonly removed from their homes at the age of seven or eight and placed in the household of a noble relative to be trained in the business of knighthood, first as a page, and later as a squire. Since Castile's upper class had long been dominated by a military mentality, one of the few occupations considered suitable for a Castilian male of noble blood was that of professional soldier. Law or commerce were deemed respectable careers for members of the Castilian middle class, but not for the proud young men of the kingdom's landed aristocracy.

Young Juan Ponce's responsibilities as a page to Núñez de Guzmán probably included serving him, his family, and guests at the table, caring for his clothing, helping him dress, cleaning, and other menial household chores. Most likely, Juan would also have cared for Don Pedro's horse and harness. In return for his labor in the house and stables of the Guzmán family, Ponce would have received instruction in social etiquette, stately ceremony, and the knightly code of honor from his master or other qualified members of his household.

By the age of 14 or 15, Ponce would have graduated to the next step in his knightly training program and become a squire. Now his instruction would expand to encompass such patrician pastimes as hunting, dancing, chess, and playing the lute (a stringed musical instrument with a pear-shaped body and a long neck). He would also have received intensive tutoring in the central tenets of the Roman Catholic faith, the dominant religion of Castile and most of the Iberian Peninsula, as well as in reading and writing. Based on what we know of the reading habits of the Castilian aristocracy, his reading probably would have included devotional (religious) works, long narrative poems relating the courageous exploits of illustrious knights such as *Poema del Cid* about the eleventh-century Castilian warrior, El Cid, and romantic odes celebrating "courtly love" between noblemen and their ladies.

Military training would have taken up the bulk of Ponce's time as a squire. Since riding was an essential skill for a knight both in combat and in tournaments (mock battles between knights), Ponce undoubtedly spent many hours perfecting his horsemanship. He also would have learned how to handle a variety of weapons from swords and daggers to long metal-tipped lances, first on foot, and later, on horseback. Juan Ponce may also have been taught to use the primitive long-guns of the period called harquebuses, although in late fifteenth-century battles, infantry (foot soldiers) were far more likely to be armed with the cumbersome and hard-to-load firearms than were knights on horseback.

The intensive military instruction Ponce would have received as a squire not only served to prepare him for his own future career as a soldier, but was also designed to help him better serve his master in tournaments and, most importantly, in the thick of battle. If Núñez de Guzmán went to war, his loyal squire Juan Ponce would be expected to follow along, taking responsibility for his master's armor, war-horse, weapons, and other equipment, and rushing to his aid if he should be injured or thrown off his mount.

In 1487, when Ponce would still have been in his teens, his military training was put to the test when he traveled to the Kingdom of Granada to fight against the Moors. Given Juan's tender age, it seems likely that he went to war in 1487 as a squire rather than as a full-fledged soldier, serving either Núñez de Guzmán or his illustrious relative from Cadiz, the great warrior Rodrigo Ponce de León. Whomever he may have served, young Juan Ponce was part of a sweeping Castilian military campaign organized by the kingdom's Roman Catholic monarchs to drive the Muslim Moors out of Granada in the southern Iberian Peninsula and back to North Africa, the land of their ancestors. The roots of the Granada campaign that provided the teenager from Santervás de Campos with his first experience of warfare reach far back into Iberian history, to the year 711, more than seven and a half centuries before Juan's birth.

By the year 711, when a force of some 20,000 Moorish conquerors crossed the Strait of Gibraltar, which separates North

Ponce de León's military apprenticeship began early, when he served as squire for the knight Don Pedro Nuñez de Guzmán. As a teenager, Ponce traveled to the Kingdom of Granada to battle the Moors, an Islamic people whose ancestors had invaded the Iberian Peninsula from Northern Africa.

Africa from the Iberian Peninsula, people had been living in what would become the nations of Portugal and Spain for tens of thousands of years, as the ancient cave paintings and engravings found throughout the peninsula testify. The Iberians, for whom the peninsula would eventually be named, probably migrated there from the south approximately 2,000 years before the birth of Jesus Christ. By about 900 B.C., the Iberians had encountered the Celts, who pushed into the peninsula from the north in several waves over the course of the next several centuries. These two peoples intermingled to become the core population of what would eventually become the interior region of the nation of Spain, and it was from these "Celtiberians" that Juan Ponce de León and most of his fellow Castilians were descended.

Over the next 16 centuries, the Iberian Peninsula's rich

mineral deposits and excellent Mediterranean and Atlantic harbors would cause it to be invaded time and time again by conquerors from three different continents. The seafaring and mercantile Phoenicians of western Asia were the first to arrive. From the heart of their trading empire on the coast of present-day Lebanon, the Phoenicians sailed westward across the Mediterranean Sea to the coast of Iberia sometime after 1000 B.C. By 900 B.C., they had established numerous trading outposts and port cities along Spain's eastern and southern shores, including the bustling Atlantic port of Gadir (later named Cadiz by the Castilians). As the Phoenicians' extensive commercial empire declined over the course of the next two centuries, Greek traders and sailors found their way to the Iberian Peninsula, creating their own commercial cities and harbors along its Mediterranean coastline.

The Phoenician and Greek conquests of Iberia were limited and largely peaceful since neither group bothered to expand their zones of influence beyond the commercial cities and towns they founded along the shores of the Atlantic and Mediterranean. The continuing conquest of Iberia took on a different character in the late second century B.C. when the peninsula became the center of a bloody military struggle between the two mightiest states of the period—Rome and Carthage. Attracted by Iberia's mines and harbors, the Carthaginians launched a military conquest of the peninsula from their capital in North Africa. By the early part of the second century B.C., Carthaginian forces controlled much of what is today eastern and southern Spain. Carthaginian rule in Iberia was to be short lived, however. Determined to crush Carthage as a commercial and military power and envious of their lucrative Iberian holdings, the rulers of Rome soon resolved to oust the Carthaginians from the peninsula and make it part of their own growing empire.

After several years of fighting, Rome vanquished its Carthaginian rival, and by 133 B.C., imperial forces had conquered most of the Iberian Peninsula. For the next five centuries, Rome would govern Iberia as a single province called Hispania.

The long Roman presence on the peninsula was destined to have a vital and enduring effect on many aspects of Spanish civilization, including philosophy, religion, law, and perhaps most of all, language, for the Spanish language developed directly from Latin, the tongue of ancient Rome.

When Rome officially adopted Catholic Christianity in the early fourth century A.D., Catholicism also became the state creed of its province, Hispania. Around the same time that Catholicism was becoming established as the dominant faith of the Iberian Peninsula, however, the vast Roman Empire was beginning to crumble. One of the chief reasons for Rome's decline was the ongoing assault on its western portion by successive waves of Germanic tribes. By the second half of the fifth century A.D., the western half of the Roman Empire had collapsed entirely and some of the Germanic invaders— particularly one tribe known as the Visigoths—had begun turning their attention toward the mineral wealth and farm-lands of Iberia. By the sixth century, Visigothic armies had swept through nearly the entire peninsula.

Hispano-Roman civilization had an enormous influence on Iberia's Germanic conquerors. Of greatest significance for the future of Spain, the Visigoth invaders soon converted to the official religion of Roman Hispania: Catholic Christianity. The Visigoths also promptly set up a centralized monarchy to rule their vast Iberian kingdom. Yet squabbling among Visigoth nobles and disputed royal successions soon weakened the Germanic tribe's hold over their new domain. By the early 700s, the way had been cleared for yet another wave of invaders to push into the Iberian Peninsula, this time from the south.

These latest conquerors were the ancestors of the Moors of Granada whom Ponce de León set off from Castile to fight nearly eight centuries later. Arab and Berber in their ethnic heritage, in their religious beliefs the Moors were ardent followers of Islam. Indeed, it was the Moors' zeal to spread their Islamic faith that inspired them to cross the Strait of Gibraltar from North Africa to Iberia in the first place.

The Moors were ardent Muslims and sought to spread their faith northward into Europe. Muslims believe Muhammad (seen here) to be the last and most important prophet sent to earth by Allah (God).

The youngest of the world's major religions, Islam was founded about A.D. 600 by an Arabian merchant named Muhammad. Muslims (as the followers of Islam are known) believe that God spoke to Muhammad through an angel, revealing to him that there is one all-powerful God and his name is Allah. The angel also informed Muhammad that he, Muhammad, was Allah's prophet. Muslims believe that Muhammad was the final and most important prophet in a long series of spiritual teachers whom Allah sent to earth to enlighten humankind, including Jesus Christ and the Hebrew patriarch Moses. Far more than just a theology, the teachings of Islam touch on all aspects of community and family life, including manners, clothing, diet, artistic expression, and legal practices.

By the time of Muhammad's death in A.D. 632, much of the Arabian Peninsula had adopted his religious teachings. Spurred on by their dynamic new faith, the Arabs burst out of their homeland to bring Islam to the rest of humankind. Soon Arab armies had converted much of western Asia and North Africa to their religion. Then in 711, the Muslim forces turned their attention northward, crossing the eight-mile wide strait separating the continent of Africa from the Iberian Peninsula.

Once they reached the peninsula, the Moors—as the Muslim invaders were dubbed by the people of Iberia—met with scant resistance from the fragmented Visigoth kingdom. Enfeebled by constant bickering over the royal succession, the Visigoth leaders could not assemble an effective and united military force. In less than a decade, the Moorish armies had managed to overrun nearly all of present-day Portugal and Spain.

The culturally and technologically sophisticated Moors introduced new agricultural techniques and crops, medical practices, mathematical concepts, and architectural styles to Iberia. They also contributed many new words to the Iberian tongue—no less than one in four modern Spanish words is of Arab origin. Yet despite the significant contributions the Moorish conquerors made to Iberian life and culture, many of the peninsula's Catholic inhabitants were grimly determined to expel the Muslim "infidels" and recover Iberia for their own people and faith. Consequently, within a few years of the Moorish invasion, "La Reconquista" (the military campaign to reclaim the Iberian Peninsula from its Muslim conquerors) was launched. The founders of the Reconquista could not have imagined just how long it would take to win back their homeland from the Moors. Dragging on for well over 700 years, the reconquest of the Iberian Peninsula was destined to be the lengthiest war in recorded history.

From the late eighth century onward, bands of Visigoths and other Catholic Christians in the mountainous far northern section of the Iberian Peninsula, a region that the Moors had largely overlooked, began organizing themselves into a fighting force. Slowly but resolutely, these Catholic warriors advanced southward into Moorish-held areas. Their campaign of reconquest was greatly aided by the Moors' inability to maintain a unified kingdom in Iberia. Around the eleventh century, quarreling among Moorish rulers led to the Muslim realm fragmenting into a number of petty kingdoms and independent cities.

Meanwhile, as the Reconquista dragged on, in northern Iberia the kingdoms of Castile and Aragon were emerging as the strongest of the various Catholic-Iberian states. With the Aragonese—and especially the large Castilian armies— spearheading the fight against the Moors, the Muslim strongholds fell one by one before the Catholic crusaders. Although the various Christian kingdoms were frequently distracted from their campaign to oust the Muslims by squabbling amongst themselves, by the late thirteenth century, they had succeeded in completely driving the Moorish "infidels" out of the narrow kingdom of Portugal on Iberia's western coast. Within the territory that would one day become Spain, only the Kingdom of Granada in the far south central portion remained under Moorish control.

For much of the next two centuries, the Moors of Granada and the Catholics who dominated the rest of the Spanish portion of the Iberian Peninsula maintained an uneasy truce. Then in 1469, around the time of Juan Ponce de León's birth, an event occurred that would prove pivotal for the Granadine Moors and the entire Iberian Peninsula: Isabella, the heir to the throne of Castile, the mightiest Spanish kingdom, married Ferdinand, the heir to the throne of Aragon, the second most powerful Spanish kingdom. Five years later, with the death of her brother, King Henry, Isabella succeeded to the crown of Castile, thereby making her husband Ferdinand king of Castile. Then in 1479, with the death of Ferdinand's father King John II, Ferdinand assumed the Aragonese throne, making Isabella queen of Aragon.

This union of crowns, however, did not entail a complete union of the two kingdoms. Aragon and Castile continued to be ruled as separate entities with their own customs and institutions (but a common foreign policy) until 1516 when Isabella and Ferdinand's grandson and heir, Carlos I merged the political institutions of the two states to form the modern nation of Spain. What the union of the Aragonese and Castilian crowns did signify, however, was that Ferdinand and Isabella together now ruled virtually all the Iberian Peninsula. Only three areas fell out of the control of the "Reyes Catolicos" (Catholic monarchs), as the king and queen were known: Portugal, ruled by its own independent monarchical government, the tiny northern Kingdom of Navarre, which would be absorbed by Aragon within a few decades, and the "infidel" Moorish Kingdom of Granada in the south.

In 1481, determined to complete the Reconquista of Spanish-Christian Iberia from the Muslims, Ferdinand and Isabella

AN ERA OF RELIGIOUS INTOLERANCE

The victory in 1492 of the Catholic forces of Isabella and Ferdinand over the Muslim armies of Granada created a surge of national patriotism within Spanish Iberia. It also launched a long period of government-sponsored religious oppression, for the Catholic monarchs clearly equated national unity with religious unity. Soon after the end of the Reconquista, Ferdinand and Isabella ordered all Jews within their realm to either convert to Catholicism or leave the Peninsula immediately. Ten years later, Spanish Iberia's only other sizable religious minority, the Muslims, were presented with the same choice by the royal government. In the meantime, the Catholic leaders of the Inquisition, a religious court established by Queen Isabella in 1478, were busily imprisoning, torturing, and executing scores of Iberian Christians (particularly recent converts from the Jewish faith) on the suspicion that they were not true adherents of Roman Catholicism.

launched an all-out military offensive against the kingdom of Granada. By the end of 1491, only the capital city of Granada remained in Moorish hands. Immediately after the start of the new year, Granada, too, capitulated to the forces of Ferdinand and Isabella, and the Catholic Reconquista of the Iberian Peninsula was finally a reality.

On January 2, 1492, Isabella and Ferdinand rode triumphantly through the streets of Granada as a jubilant throng of Reconquista veterans saluted and cheered the Catholic monarchs. Almost certainly, Ponce de León was in the exuberant crowd that gathered that day in the former Moorish capital to celebrate the great Catholic victory over the Muslim "infidels." Yet even as he rejoiced with his fellow comrades-in-arms over the successful conclusion of the bloody crusade that had preoccupied Christian Iberia for nearly a millennium, Ponce must also have entertained more than a few doubts about his own future, now that the fighting was done.

Juan Ponce may have come from an aristocratic background, but he seems to have possessed no wealth of his own. In their histories, both Oviedo and Las Casas describe young Ponce as poor. That Juan was impoverished despite his noble parentage probably had a great deal to do with his birth order within his family. Most likely, Ponce had the misfortune of being born a second or third son. According to the customs of fifteenth-century Castile—and indeed, of most of Western Europe during this period—only the eldest son of a noble stood to inherit any property upon the death of his parent. Known as primogeniture, this practice may seem unjust to us today, but it served an important purpose in a society in which wealth and status were based primarily on land ownership. By passing along their entire holdings to one heir, noblemen ensured that their estates would remain intact, and therefore, economically viable. Unless he owned a great deal of property, a noble who split his land among a number of heirs would end up impoverishing all of his offspring and gravely diminishing the influence and prestige of the family name.

Keenly aware that he would not be inheriting his father's estate, Ponce had undoubtedly planned on carving out a career for himself as a professional soldier. As of late 1491, his résumé for a successful martial career looked promising: he had received his early military training from a distinguished warrior—Don Pedro Núñez de Guzmán, Knight Commander of the Order of Calatrava—and had gained plenty of firsthand battlefield experience during a half-decade of fighting the Moors. With the final defeat of the Moorish forces in January 1492, however, what the aspiring career soldier from Santervás de Campos lacked was a military campaign. The Reconquista had employed—and often enriched by means of government-sanctioned plundering of the enemy—countless generations of Castilians and other Christian Iberians. Now the long conflict was finally over, and like thousands of others among his fellow Reconquista veterans, Ponce faced a very uncertain future in his homeland.

Although Ponce and the other unemployed soldiers who gathered on the streets of Granada on January 2, 1492 could not have known it, an exciting new opportunity was waiting for them. For before the year was over, an obscure but determined navigator from Genoa, a city in the north of what is now the Italian Republic, named Christopher Columbus would sail 3,000 miles across the Atlantic Ocean and discover what was for the people of the Iberian Peninsula and the rest of Europe, a completely "New World." By claiming the new land across the Atlantic for the Castilian crown, Columbus would make it the object—and the salvation—of Juan Ponce de León and an entire generation of Spanish conquistadors and fortune-seekers.

3

Journey to a New World

On August 3, 1492, almost seven months to the day after the fall of Granada, Christopher Columbus departed the Castilian port of Palos on the Gulf of Cadiz to sail westward across the Atlantic. Like the majority of his compatriots, Juan Ponce de León probably had no knowledge of the Italian mariner's daring expedition, although his own sovereigns were sponsoring the voyage. Ponce would probably have been aware, however, of the key commercial motivations that spurred Columbus' momentous journey in the summer of 1492, and of at least some of the technological advances that made the explorer's transatlantic voyage possible in the first place.

A craving for adventure and glory, a zeal to convert heathens to the Christian faith, and simple curiosity were among the motives that prompted Columbus and other intrepid Europeans to take to the sea and "discover" (at least for other Europeans) distant regions of the globe during the late 1400s and early 1500s. Yet most historians agree that the chief impetus for Europe's so-called "Age of Discovery" was

On August 3, 1492, Italian explorer Christopher Columbus (depicted in this painting as he kisses the hand of his patron, Queen Isabella) set out on the first of his voyages across the Atlantic. Spain's Queen Isabella funded the expedition in the hope of opening new trade routes to Asia and spreading Christianity to distant peoples.

commercial. It was the search for new trade routes, and specifically for new ways to reach Asian markets, that more than any other factor spurred the great transoceanic explorations of Columbus' era.

Well before Ponce's birth, prosperous Castilians and other Europeans had acquired a strong taste for Asian goods. Eastern luxuries including precious stones and metals, fine silks, and exotic spices had been familiar items in the West since the days of ancient Rome when imperial merchants had conducted an extensive and lucrative trade with Asia. Ginger, cloves, cinnamon, nutmeg, pepper, and other Eastern spices were particularly valued by Europeans. In an era without refrigeration, these aromatic bits of leaves, seeds, and barks helped to mask the disagreeable tastes and odors of rancid meat. They also added new interest to a diet centered on such bland fare as parsnips, cabbage, porridge, and bread.

After the fall of the Roman Empire, trade between Asia and the politically fragmented and war-ridden European continent dwindled. Those Asian goods that did manage to make their way to the cities and towns of Europe during the early Middle Ages were typically obtained through intermediaries in the Middle East, and were prohibitively expensive. Western merchants began to search for ways to avoid the Arab middlemen and their costly mark-ups.

From about the middle of the thirteenth century to the middle of the fourteenth century, a handful of European traders seeking direct contacts with Eastern merchants boldly trekked overland through central Asia to India and China. During that period, central Asia was under the rule of the Mongols, a nomadic Asian people who were amicable toward Westerners. The most famous of the enterprising European merchants to make the arduous journey east across Mongol territory was Marco Polo of the Italian city-state of Venice. Polo spent 18 years in China serving as an official in the court of the legendary Mongol ruler Kublai Khan before returning home and writing a wildly popular account of his adventures in the exotic East entitled *Description of the World.*

The overland route to eastern Asia blazed by Polo and other medieval merchants, however, became too dangerous for even the most intrepid Western travelers in the late 1300s when the Mongol Empire that had long brought peace to central Asia began to disintegrate. The plight of European merchants seeking Asian goods worsened further during the first half of the fifteenth century when a Muslim and fervently anti-Christian dynasty—the Turkish Ottomans—took advantage of the power vacuum created by the collapsing Mongol Empire to carve out a vast empire of their own stretching from the Balkan Peninsula to western Asia and North Africa.

By the mid-1400s, various Muslim groups—Turkish and Arab—possessed a stranglehold on both the overland routes and the traditional sea routes connecting Europe to eastern Asia. Exorbitant mark-ups by the Muslim intermediaries as well as by Venetian merchants whose city-state on the Adriatic Sea served as the entry point for virtually all Asian goods brought to Europe, meant that Eastern spices and silks were more costly than ever in the West. Once again, frustrated European merchants began to ponder the possibility of finding new routes to Asia's riches, routes that would bypass the troublesome Muslims—and Venetians—altogether. Convinced that a viable new overland route to the East did not exist, this time they focused on the sea.

Europeans not only possessed a strong incentive for ocean-going exploration—the discovery of new oceanic highways to the East—but also the technological means to realize their goal by the late 1400s. Over the course of the previous centuries, Western sailors had steadily refined their navigational techniques and equipment. More accurate maps and a better understanding of oceanic wind patterns, combined with the development of navigational instruments such as the magnetic compass and the astrolabe (which helped determine latitude by pinpointing the position of the sun or stars), meant that Europeans could now confidently undertake longer sea voyages than ever before.

The invention of new, more seaworthy vessels also contributed to the birth of Europe's Age of Discovery. The most important of these sailing ships was the caravella (caravel). This sturdy yet swift three-masted craft was particularly well suited to long ocean voyages because it was both maneuverable enough to sail against the wind and roomy enough to accommodate a substantial amount of provisions and trade goods.

The first European state to use these technological advances in ship design and navigation to seek a new water route to Asia was Castile's western neighbor on the Iberian Peninsula, Portugal. That Portugal should have taken the lead in launching Europe's great age of oceangoing exploration is hardly surprising considering that the Atlantic Ocean borders its entire western and southern shores. Moreover, although Portugal, like the rest of Iberia, was conquered by the Moors in 711, its armies had managed to expel the Muslim invaders by the mid-1200s, more than two centuries before the Spanish Iberians completed their Reconquista. Secure within its own borders and under the able leadership of a strong, centralized monarchy, Portugal could afford to turn its attention outward, toward the Atlantic Ocean and beyond.

PORTUGAL VERSUS SPAIN

In the fifteenth century, the pope, as head of the Catholic Church, was supposed to approve the claim of any European state to an unoccupied, non-Christian territory. After 1492, Portugal and Castile became rivals for heathen lands around the world. In 1493, Pope Alexander VI legalized Ferdinand and Isabella's claim to the lands discovered by Columbus and to all lands approximately 350 miles west of the Portuguese-occupied Cape Verde Islands in the Atlantic. This ruling meant that Africa and India fell within Portugal's zone of influence, but the entire New World went to the Catholic monarchs. The following year, in the Treaty of Tordesillas, Ferdinand and Isabella agreed to shift the imaginary line running through the Atlantic nearly 1,000 miles farther west, meaning that Brazil (which would be discovered in 1500) would become Portuguese, but that Spain would be able to claim the rest of South and Central America in addition to the Caribbean islands in the years ahead.

By the middle of the fifteenth century, Portuguese sea captains had begun pushing down Africa's western coast in hopes of finding a way to what Europeans called the "Indies" (modern-day Japan, China, India, Indonesia, and Southeast Asia) by rounding the continent's southernmost point, then veering eastward. Over a period of several decades, Portuguese vessels made their way farther and farther down Africa's long Atlantic shoreline, picking up valuable cargoes of ivory, gold dust, and slaves along the way. Finally, in 1488, the Portuguese navigator Bartolomeu Dias rounded the Cape of Good Hope at Africa's extreme tip and sailed into the Indian Ocean, showing the way for his compatriot, Vasco da Gama, to follow from the Portuguese city of Lisbon all the way to India in 1497.

While Portuguese navigators were trying to reach the Indies by venturing ever farther south along Africa's Atlantic coastline, Christopher Columbus was arriving at the startling conclusion that a quicker route to Asia lay due west of Europe. In 1484, four years before Bartolomeu Dias sighted the Cape of Good Hope, Columbus tried to convince the Portuguese king to back his "Enterprise of the Indies," as he dubbed his plan to get to the East by sailing west across the Atlantic. The king refused, for most scholars of the day argued (quite correctly) that Columbus had vastly underestimated the circumference of the earth, on the one hand, and vastly overestimated the size of the Asian continent, on the other. Attempting to sail west to Asia was impractical, they said—the distance between Europe's western coast and Asia's eastern shores was simply too great to be safely traversed by sailing ship.

Columbus next took his idea to King Ferdinand and Queen Isabella. Still in the final throes of their campaign to drive the Moors from Granada, the rulers were unable to devote serious attention to his scheme. Columbus, however, refused to give up. His persistence paid off in January 1492 when Ferdinand and Isabella, in an expansive and self-confident mood following the surrender of Granada, agreed to take a chance on the stubborn Italian navigator and his unorthodox plan.

The Catholic monarchs had a variety of motives for backing Columbus' Enterprise of the Indies. Should Columbus indeed discover a rapid new means of reaching Asian markets, establishing direct trade ties with Eastern merchants would surely prove to be highly lucrative for their kingdoms. The voyage to India by Portuguese navigator Vasco da Gama was still five years in the future, and Ferdinand and Isabella must have realized that if Columbus found a deepwater route to the Indies before their Iberian neighbor or any other European rival, as his sponsors, they would hold a monopoly on the profitable Asian-European trade. Moreover, Columbus might find gold or other sources of mineral wealth in the lands he discovered on his westward voyage. Finally, the Catholic monarchs reasoned, the heathen peoples Columbus might encounter on his expedition would provide them with an extraordinary opportunity to fulfill what they viewed as one of their chief duties as Catholic rulers: bringing Christianity to those who had not yet had a chance to hear its message and be saved.

Following months of negotiations with the Catholic monarchs regarding the nature of his compensation should his "Enterprise" prove successful, on August 3, 1492, Columbus and a fleet of three vessels departed the Gulf of Cadiz in southern Castile for the open Atlantic. About two months later, on October 12, Columbus made landfall on one of the small outlying islands of the island group known today as the Bahamas. After naming the island San Salvador (Our Savior), Columbus solemnly claimed it for his royal sponsors.

On San Salvador, Columbus encountered his first native Americans. Members of the largest ethnic group in the Caribbean—the Taino—the islanders were friendly and docile, according to Columbus, who noted in his log that they "ought to make good and skilled servants." Confident that he was somewhere in the Indies, Columbus dubbed the people he found on the islands of the Caribbean Basin "Indios" (Indians), and the peoples of the Americas—from South America all the way into what is now Canada—were given this general and inaccurate label. Indeed,

Two months after sailing from Castile, Columbus landed on an island that is today part of the Bahamas (a chain of small islands that stretches southeast off the coast of Florida), and quickly claimed it in the name of Spain. Exploring other islands of the Caribbean, Columbus encountered many native peoples, whom he called "Indios," believing that he had arrived in the Far East, near India.

throughout three additional New World voyages and right up until his death in 1506, Columbus never gave up his conviction that the territories he discovered were in the Far East. Little could he have known that the lands he had found were nearly 10,000 miles from the Indies, with the vast American continents obstructing the way between. (Sometime during the ninth or tenth centuries A.D., Vikings from Iceland and Greenland made their way to the eastern coast of North America in small, open boats, but by Columbus' time, the Norsemen's discovery of the American continent had long been forgotten.)

Upon leaving San Salvador, Columbus sailed southwest to Cuba, and from there to another big island he called the Isle of Spain, a name that has come down to us as Hispaniola. (Today, the island of Hispaniola is home to two different nations—Haiti in the west and the Dominican Republic in the east.) Off the coast of Hispaniola, Columbus lost his flagship, the *Santa María*, when the vessel struck a coral reef on Christmas Eve. Determined to make the best of this misfortune, Columbus salvaged lumber from the wrecked ship to construct a fort on the shores of Hispaniola, which he named La Navidad (Nativity or Christmas). Thirty-nine of Columbus' 90-man crew agreed to stay behind at La Navidad. Until Columbus could return for them, they were to explore the island further for gold deposits and, if possible, trade with the native peoples for the precious metal. Columbus was hopeful that the men would be successful in their efforts to obtain gold since a number of Taino he had encountered on the island sported gold earrings or nose rings.

In January 1493, Columbus started the long voyage home, bringing with him half a dozen "Indians," several colorful parrots, and the modest amount of gold—most of it in the form of jewelry or ornaments—he had been able to obtain from the natives in exchange for glass beads, bells, and other trinkets. Columbus must have been gratified by the warm reception he received two months later in the court of Ferdinand and Isabella. Apparently convinced that Columbus had indeed reached the Indies and captivated by his promises of the gold and other potential natural wealth that was sure to be uncovered in the lands he had found, the Catholic monarchs fulfilled an earlier pledge to grant Columbus the hereditary titles of "Admiral of the Ocean Seas," governor general, and viceroy of all discovered territories. In addition to these honors, Columbus was to receive

10 percent of any profits taken from the new lands he reached. Ferdinand and Isabella also promptly agreed to Columbus' request for a second and much larger expedition to relieve the sailors left behind on Hispaniola and settle additional colonists there to mine and trade with the natives for gold and other precious commodities. During the second expedition, Hispaniola was also to be used as a base by Columbus for additional exploration in search of China and the rest of the Asian mainland and of new and unclaimed lands.

Even before Columbus set foot in the royal court to report to his sponsors, news of his dramatic voyage of exploration had spread throughout the Iberian Peninsula and into the rest of Europe. Published accounts of the expedition made the lands Columbus had found appear very attractive—supposedly, they overflowed with gold, precious stones, and exotic spices and were inhabited by peaceful natives who were sure to make compliant servants. Lured by the promise of quick wealth, hundreds of Castilian men eagerly signed up for Columbus' planned return voyage. Among them was a young soldier named Juan Ponce de León.

On the morning of September 25, 1493, Columbus' second voyage west departed from the port of Cadiz amidst great fanfare. One of Ponce's fellow passengers described the 17-vessel fleet's spectacular send-off from Castile in a letter to an acquaintance:

> The religious rites usual on such occasions were performed by the sailors; the last embraces were given by those setting out on the voyage; the ships were hung with banners; streamers were flying from the rigging; the royal standard [of Castile] flew at the stern of every ship. . . . The shores echoed the blare of trumpets and the blasting of horns, and even the sea bottom echoed the canon's roar.

Much larger than the expedition that had set out from Castile a little more than a year earlier, Columbus' second voyage carried some 1,200 to 1,500 passengers—all of them male, since by royal command no women were permitted to participate in the voyage. Ponce's shipmates included several hundred foot soldiers and one cavalry troop to help explore the new lands and provide protection for the entire enterprise, skilled craftsmen, merchants, and farmers to settle the new territories and trade with the natives for gold and other valuable items, and six Catholic priests, who were charged with converting the heathen Indians to Christianity. With the exception of the priests and a group of 200 "gentlemen volunteers," all the men were salaried employees of the crown.

Although the name Juan Ponce de León does not appear on any of the ship rosters or other records of the voyage that have survived over the centuries, there is substantial evidence for Ponce's participation in the expedition, either as a soldier on the royal payroll or as one of the "gentlemen volunteers." The two chief historians of the early Spanish colonial period in the New World, Bartolomé de las Casas and Gonzalo Fernández de Oviedo, place Ponce on Columbus' second voyage, and both men were in an excellent position to know. Oviedo, by his own admission, was well acquainted with Ponce, having met him in Spain some two decades after the 1493 voyage. Las Casas was also a personal acquaintance of Ponce, having spent time with him in Hispaniola in the early 1500s. Moreover, although Las Casas himself did not travel to the New World until 1502, his father Pedro, a merchant, and three of his uncles were passengers on Columbus' second expedition, and may well have told Las Casas that they had voyaged across the Atlantic with Juan Ponce in 1493.

According to Las Casas, Ponce voyaged to the New World in the autumn of 1493 as a "peón" (foot soldier). Yet Robert Fuson and other modern scholars believe that in light of his aristocratic background, it is more likely that Ponce was among the 200 gentlemen volunteers on board. Unlike the soldiers, who were employees of the crown, the gentlemen volunteers had to buy their way onto the expedition. Surely this would have presented a significant problem for the impoverished Ponce. Nonetheless, speculates Fuson, one of Ponce's wealthy and

Although the name of Ponce de León does not appear on the crew rosters of Columbus' second voyage, historian Bartolomé de Las Casas places Ponce as part of the expedition. This view is supported by the fact that several of Las Casas' relatives, including his father, are known to have been on the ship and could have told Las Casas that Ponce was also aboard.

influential relatives—of whom he had several in Cadiz, the port of departure—could easily have picked up the tab for him.

Assuming Fuson is right about how Ponce obtained a place in Columbus' expedition, it seems probable that Juan was not the only gentleman volunteer on board being subsidized by well-off relatives. Most historians agree that the ranks of the gentlemen volunteers on Columbus' second voyage were largely filled by financially strapped members of Castile's lesser nobility or hidalgo class. Like Ponce, many of the hidalgos on Columbus' second voyage had probably fought in the recent war against the Moors and had found themselves out of a job with the fall of Granada in January 1492. It seems logical to assume that the majority of these hidalgo volunteers were second or third sons, as Ponce de León almost certainly was, and stood to inherit little or nothing from their fathers. Eldest sons of propertied parents, after all, had scant incentive to make the long and risky voyage across the Atlantic. Younger sons, in contrast, had nothing to lose and potentially, a great deal to gain by going to the New World where they could stake out a claim to some of the new lands' reputed riches. Many of these hidalgo adventurers did not plan to settle permanently across the sea, but rather dreamed of securing a personal fortune in the new lands as quickly as possible, then returning home to Castile to enjoy their winnings.

Along with its human cargo of gentlemen adventurers, priests, soldiers, artisans, and farmers, Columbus' 17 vessels carried provisions for the voyage and the first several months of settlement, armaments such as crossbows and harquebuses, hoes, pickaxes, and other tools, and a wide variety of seeds, plants, and livestock for establishing Spanish-style agriculture in the New World. Among the numerous animals on board were goats, sheep, cattle, pigs, chickens, and horses. "In short," notes the historian Zvi Dor-Ner, "the fleet bore a portable Europe in its holds, a Europe that would never leave the Americas from that day to this."

Loaded down with supplies, livestock, and passengers, the vessels of Columbus' second expedition must have provided little breathing room for Ponce and his fellow travelers. Aside from their cramped quarters, Ponce and the other passengers probably would have found plenty to complain about in the shipboard fare. A staple of every shipboard meal of the era was the infamous ship's biscuit or hardtack, small loaves of bread twice- or thrice-baked to thoroughly dry them out and prevent them from spoiling at sea. Since insect infestations were a constant problem on ships, by a week or so into the voyage, the ship's biscuit and much of the other food stored on board was typically crawling with weevils (a type of beetle). Aside from the weevils, the passengers' and crews' other chief source of protein were tough chunks of pork, beef, and fish, soaked in brine and packed away in wooden barrels as a means of preservation. For the main meal of the day, the chewy pickled meat and fish were usually combined with dried peas or beans to make a simple and undoubtedly quite unappetizing stew. To wash down the stale ship's biscuit and salty meat there was wine or water, which often spoiled in the casks it was kept in long before the voyage was completed. Regarding the drinking water on his ship, a Spaniard who sailed to the New World along the same route as Ponce some years later grumbled: "It is necessary to lose your senses of taste and smell and sight just to drink it."

Seasickness added greatly to the discomfort of many travelers who crossed the Atlantic in wooden sailing ships during the fifteenth and sixteenth centuries. No doubt, motion sicknesses was a particular problem for landlubbers like young Juan Ponce, who hailed from the interior region of his country and would have had little—if any—prior experience with sea travel. The same Spanish voyager who found his vessel's water supply so repugnant described in vivid detail the wrenching bouts of nausea that gripped him and his shipmates as their sailing ship pitched and rolled across the Atlantic:

> They put us in a tiny chamber that was three palms high and five palms square, in which, as we entered, the force of the sea did such violence to our stomachs and heads, that, parents and children, old and young, we turned the color of corpses, and we commenced . . . to say "baac, baac," and after that "bor, bor, bor, bor," together spewing from our mouths all that had entered therein that day and the preceding one. . . . In this manner we continued without seeing sun nor moon, nor did we open our eyes, nor change our clothing from when we entered the cabin, nor even more, until the third day at sea . . .

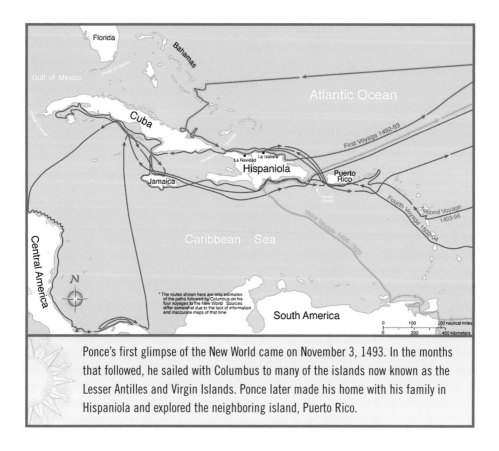

Ponce's first glimpse of the New World came on November 3, 1493. In the months that followed, he sailed with Columbus to many of the islands now known as the Lesser Antilles and Virgin Islands. Ponce later made his home with his family in Hispaniola and explored the neighboring island, Puerto Rico.

After three weeks on the open sea, Ponce and his fellow travelers must have been greatly relieved to hear the cry, "Tierra! Tierra!" ("Land, Land") shortly after dawn on Sunday, November 3, 1493. That morning, Ponce received his first glimpse of the New World when the fleet sighted two small islands in the Caribbean archipelago known today as the Lesser Antilles. After naming the islands Dominica (Latin for Sunday or "Our Lord's Day" after the day of the week on which it was discovered) and Santa María la Gallante (after the expedition's flagship), Columbus claimed the new land for Isabella and Ferdinand. The fleet then sailed north and west through the rest of the Lesser Antilles and the Virgin Islands, reaching the mountainous southern coast of a picturesque island the native peoples called Borinquén (Land of the Great Lords) on November 19. Although Columbus dubbed the island San Juan

Bautista (Saint John the Baptist), ultimately it would be renamed Puerto Rico (Rich Port), after its first port city. Ponce could not have guessed it at the time, but the island of Puerto Rico would play a significant role in his future life in the New World.

From Puerto Rico, the fleet hastened to the northern coast of Hispaniola, where Columbus had left 39 men nearly one year ago on his first voyage. Columbus was eager to see how the men at La Navidad had fared. Had they found the gold mines he had assured King Ferdinand and Queen Isabella existed on the island? And how had their efforts to establish trade with the locals gone? Surely after almost a year of living side by side with the Tainos of Hispaniola, the Castilians would have been able to build a lucrative trade with the Indians for precious metals, gems, spices, and any number of other valuable and exotic commodities. As Columbus' fleet drew nearer to "the Isle of Spain," Ponce and his shipmates, most of whom had been lured into making the voyage by the promise of easy wealth, must have been filled with anticipation. What Ponce de León and his fellow voyagers found on shore, however, would dismay them.

Colonization
of Hispaniola

While the fleet was still about 20 miles east of the garrison the crew of Columbus' first voyage had constructed the previous Christmas on Hispaniola, a shore party scouting for potential sites for new settlements made a grisly discovery: four dead Spaniards, their rotting corpses bound together with a rope. An alarmed Columbus headed his fleet immediately for La Navidad. Arriving at nightfall, he lit flares and fired a cannon to alert the men on land of his arrival. From the darkened shore, there came only an eerie silence.

Early the next morning, Columbus and a heavily armed landing party found the fort at La Navidad reduced to ashes and a number of decomposing bodies scattered nearby. It soon became painfully evident that there were no survivors. Nor were there any gold or precious gems in La Navidad, as Columbus and his group were forced to conclude after spending many hours digging under the ruined garrison.

Guacanagarí, the local Taino cacique (a hereditary chief who usually ruled several neighboring villages), had established friendly

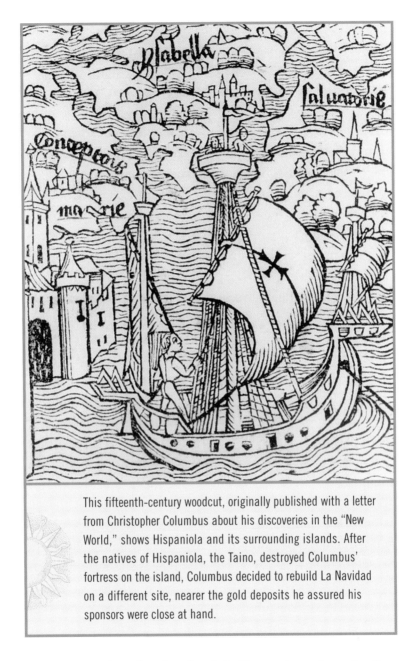

This fifteenth-century woodcut, originally published with a letter from Christopher Columbus about his discoveries in the "New World," shows Hispaniola and its surrounding islands. After the natives of Hispaniola, the Taino, destroyed Columbus' fortress on the island, Columbus decided to rebuild La Navidad on a different site, nearer the gold deposits he assured his sponsors were close at hand.

relations with Columbus back in December when the fort was constructed. After spotting Columbus' landing party, Guacanagarí hurried to the site of the charred outpost to fill the admiral in on what had happened over the past year. He told Columbus of how some of the Spaniards, frustrated in their efforts to find gold deposits near La Navidad, had set off for the domain of another cacique named Caonabó. There they had abducted and raped a number of native women and compelled the men to help them hunt for gold. Goaded into violence by the foreigners' ruthless treatment of his people, Caonabó marshaled his forces and ambushed the invaders. Then he led his men to La Navidad to kill the rest of the Spaniards and burn down their fortress. Guacanagarí and his people tried to help the Spaniards, the cacique told Columbus, but were beaten back by Caonabó's warriors.

After toying with the idea of rebuilding La Navidad, Columbus determined to found a new base in Hispaniola, one that would hopefully prove to be closer to the elusive gold deposits he had convinced his sponsors—and himself—existed somewhere on the large island. At the end of December, Columbus broke ground for a new colony about 30 miles east of La Navidad on Hispaniola's northern coast, naming it La Isabella after the queen. Keenly aware that the native peoples he described in his log as "cowardly" when he first came to the New World were not nearly as timid as he had once imagined, Columbus ordered that a high wall be erected around the settlement and sentinels stationed day and night. After the wall was finished, the new colonists set to work fashioning crude shelters for themselves. "[W]e made two hundred houses, which are as small as hunting cabins back home and are roofed with grass," wrote one of Ponce's fellow expedition members. By late January 1494, the first permanent Spanish settlement in the Western Hemisphere had been completed.

It is at this point that Juan Ponce de León disappears from any of the existing documents or accounts of either the New World or the Old World. His name does not reappear in the historical record until eight years later, in 1502, when Las Casas reports that Ponce traveled with him from Castile to Hispaniola as part of the fleet carrying the island's newly appointed governor across the Atlantic. Obviously, Ponce must have returned to Castile at some point between 1494 and 1502, but no one knows exactly when or why. It is possible that he left Hispaniola as early as February 1494 when 12 of Columbus' original 17 vessels were sent home to pick up much-needed supplies for the fledgling colony, including food, tools, medicine, and clothing.

Historians know that a number of the prospective colonists returned to Iberia on the 12-vessel fleet in the winter of 1494. Most of them probably went home because of illness, for the new settlement of La Navidad was a sickly place. Unfortunately, Columbus had picked a poor location for his town—too close to coastal marshes and the swarms of insects they bred and too far from a good source of fresh water. The combination of a hot damp climate, inadequate and often spoiled food and water, hard physical labor, and disease-carrying mosquitoes caused hundreds of settlers to fall sick. Perhaps Ponce was one of those who were stricken during that difficult first winter and decided to return home for medical treatment.

Whenever Ponce may have left the New World, according to Las Casas, he returned there in April 1502 as one of the approximately 2,500 colonists, soldiers, and adventurers who traveled across the ocean with Hispaniola's newly appointed governor, Don Fray Nicolás de Ovando. The roots of the monarchs' decision to assign a new governor for Hispaniola, although Columbus, according to his earlier agreements with the crown was supposed to serve as governor for life of all the lands he discovered, go back to the earliest years of Spanish settlement on the island.

From the beginning, Columbus was an ineffective and unpopular colonial administrator. The "Admiral of the Ocean Seas," most of his biographers agree, was far less competent and resourceful as a governor than he was as a navigator. During his frequent absences from Hispaniola on exploratory voyages in the Caribbean, Columbus left the island under the care of his two brothers, who proved as inept at administration as the admiral himself. Yet, even if they had possessed stronger leadership skills, Columbus and his brothers would still have faced daunting challenges in directing the island's political and economic affairs. For one thing, Columbus and his siblings were natives of Genoa on the Italian peninsula, and the island's predominantly Spanish colonists disliked being ordered around by foreigners. For another, many of the settlers felt personally betrayed by the admiral's promises of easy wealth in the New World. Bitterly disappointed by the meager supply of gold and other valuable commodities they had been able to locate on Hispaniola, they resented Columbus for exaggerating the island's mineral riches after he returned to Europe from his first voyage in 1493.

Whereas the obvious discrepancy between New World realities and Columbus' grandiose claims regarding the lands he had found across the Atlantic angered colonists who had come to Hispaniola to make their fortunes, the governor's brutal treatment of the native islanders incensed priests who had come there to save Indian souls. Desperate to obtain more gold to impress his sponsors and shore up his foundering New World enterprise, Columbus compelled all Tainos over 14 years of age to provide him with a set amount of gold dust every three months. If an Indian proved unable or unwilling to pay the levy, he faced severe punishment, including having his hands cut off or execution.

Forced to spend much of their days frantically panning streams and rivers for tiny fragments of gold to meet the admiral's quotas, the Tainos were hard pressed to find the time to tend their crops, fish, or hunt. With their normal production of food severely disrupted, many Indians on Hispaniola went hungry. When the Tainos finally revolted against the cruel quota system, Columbus responded by instituting a labor arrangement that stopped little short of slavery, in which groups of Indians were assigned to particular settlers to toil for them as miners, agricultural workers, or servants.

Back in the royal court, a steady stream of returned colonists and priests complained to the king and queen about what they viewed as Columbus' mismanagement of Hispaniola and demanded an investigation. Finally, the Catholic monarchs decided they had to act. In 1500, they sent a commissioner named

To justify his claims of great wealth in the New World, Columbus pressed the native inhabitants into grueling service. Far less adept as an administrator than as a navigator, Columbus demanded that each of the local Tainos over the age of 14 present him with a certain amount of gold dust every three months. Penalties for non-compliance were severe.

Francisco de Bobadilla to Hispaniola to look into the charges against Columbus. On discovering that seven insubordinate Spanish colonists had just been executed by order of Columbus' government, an incensed Bobadilla had the admiral and his brothers arrested and sent to Castile in chains for trial.

Convinced that their commissioner had gone too far, the Catholic monarchs were embarrassed by Bobadilla's harsh treatment of the famed explorer. After pardoning Columbus, they restored his hereditary titles and all the property Bobadilla had confiscated from him in Hispaniola following his arrest. Yet, if Ferdinand and Isabella believed that Bobadilla had been overzealous in his punishment of Columbus, the admiral nonetheless had irrevocably lost the trust of his royal sponsors. Never again would Columbus be permitted to take any significant role in the government of Hispaniola or any of the other New World lands he had discovered. He was still technically "Admiral of the Ocean Seas," governor general, and viceroy of all the territories he had claimed for Ferdinand and Isabella, but from now on Columbus' high-sounding titles were to be bereft of any actual authority.

In early 1502, Ferdinand and Isabella decided to give the task of restoring order and unity to Hispaniola to an experienced Castilian administrator and soldier, the aristocratic Nicolas de Ovando, knight-commander of the Order of Lares. In April 1502, the new governor's 30-ship fleet arrived at Santo Domingo on the southern coast of Hispaniola, the island's chief port since its founding in 1494. As soon as the fleet anchored in Santo Domingo harbor, Las Casas reports, he overheard several of his shipmates eagerly calling to the men gathered on shore, " 'What news? What news is there of the land?' 'Good news, good news!' came the reply.... 'There is a war with the Indians, so there will be plenty of slaves!' " As Las Casas and his traveling companion Juan Ponce de León would soon discover, the new war with the Indians that so pleased their compatriots was being fought in the sole part of the island that had not been subjugated by 1502, the far eastern-most region known as Higüey.

The trouble in Higüey had started a few weeks earlier when a dog belonging to a Spanish official had attacked and killed a local cacique. The Indians who witnessed the ferocious assault were convinced that the official had deliberately set the dog on their chief. The brutal incident appalled and outraged the entire Taino community. Determined to avenge the death of his fellow leader, a powerful Higüey chieftain named Cotubanama commanded his warriors to ambush and kill a party of eight Spaniards who happened to be passing through his territory.

Upon taking office in the middle of April 1502, one of Governor Ovando's very first acts was to organize an army to go after Cotubanama and his rebellious followers on Hispaniola's eastern frontier. Apparently, Ovando believed that he could not put the island's political and economic affairs into order until all of Hispaniola's native peoples had been subjugated. The large military expedition Ovando sent to Higüey included many of the new colonists who came with him to the New World, and it seems likely that the trained soldier Juan Ponce de León would have been among them. Although the Indians greatly outnumbered the Spaniards, the Taino warriors were armed with crude and largely ineffective weapons including rocks, wooden clubs, and arrows tipped with sharpened fish bones. Equipped with steel swords, lances, crossbows, firearms, and specially trained war dogs, Ovando's forces conquered the rebellious natives with merciless efficiency. Hundreds of Indians were wounded or killed in the fighting, and at least as many were taken as slaves, according to Las Casas, who accompanied the troops to Higüey, possibly as a military provisioner.

Despite the rapidity and brutality with which the Spaniards quelled the Tainos' first uprising in Higüey, by 1504 the province's indigenous peoples were again challenging Spanish authority by refusing to transport cassava (sometimes called manioc) bread from their villages to the large Spanish settlement in Santo Domingo. Hispaniola's Spanish settlers, and especially those in the island's bigger towns like Santo Domingo, depended almost entirely on the Indians to grow and produce the food they required. Eastern Hispaniola, bereft of gold deposits but blessed with plenty of fertile farmland, soon emerged as an important agricultural center for the colonists. In particular, the Spaniards depended on Higüey as a major source of cultivated cassava and the filling bread made from the roots of that bushy, stiff-leafed plant. Carbohydrate- and vitamin-rich, cassava bread has a shelf life of over a year and was a staple of both the Tainos' and the Spanish colonists' diets. Early on in their colonization efforts, the Spaniards of Santo Domingo hit on the idea of having Higüey's natives pay a regular tribute to them of the nutritious bread.

Producing cassava bread was a complex undertaking for the Taino. First the cassava plants had to be harvested. Then their

In Hispaniola, the Spanish colonists relied on the local Taino people to provide them with food. A staple of the Taino diet is cassava bread, a carbohydrate- and vitamin-rich food made from the roots of the indigenous cassava plant. Though poisonous in its natural form, cassava was peeled, juiced, and grated before being baked over hot stones to remove any toxins.

fleshy, white roots had to be carefully processed to render them into edible flour, a time-consuming and exhausting procedure. The reason cassava flour is so difficult to process is because the tubers of the plant from which it is derived contain a highly poisonous substance known as hydrocyanic (prussic) acid. Making the cassava roots safe for consumption involved pounding them with heavy stones, then peeling, grating, and squeezing the tubers to remove as much of their toxic juices as possible.

The starchy pulp that was left was then heated to dry it into flour. Then, a dough was formed by mixing the flour with water, and the batter shaped into large, flat breads, which like tortillas, could be stuffed with meat, fish, or vegetables before eating. When the cassava bread was grilled on stones over a hot fire, whatever small amount of toxic compounds remaining in the batter despite all the painstaking crushing, shredding, and squeezing of the roots were rendered harmless by the cooking process.

Spurred on by their leader, Cotubanama, the Indians of Higüey began refusing to convey the cassava bread they had so laboriously prepared to Santo Domingo, nearly 100 miles away, in defiance of the Spaniards' directives. The colonists, they apparently figured, could at least make the effort to get themselves to Higüey to pick up the tribute rather than making the already overtaxed natives take additional time from caring for their own fields and families to transport the bread. As the new colonial administration was pondering how to respond to the insubordinate Tainos, an incident occurred in the province that convinced Ovando to make war once again on the people of Higüey.

Following the defeat of the Tainos in the first uprising, the Spaniards, who as yet had no permanent settlements in Higüey, built a token garrison in an Indian village near the coast. Before long, the small but well-armed group of Spanish soldiers assigned to guard the fort began abducting and raping the local women and bullying the men. In retaliation, a band of Taino warriors ambushed and burned the fort, killing nine of the ten soldiers stationed there. One Spaniard, who managed to escape by pretending to be dead, made his way to Santo Domingo to alert the governor of what had taken place in Higüey. Determined to subjugate the belligerent Tainos of eastern Hispaniola once and for all, Ovando ordered the organization of an invading force composed of several hundred men from each of the island's major Spanish settlements. Commanding the force from Santo Domingo was Captain Juan Ponce de León.

As in the case of the first Indian war in Higüey, Las Casas' detailed account of the second conflict indicates he must have accompanied the troops to battle. In his chronicle of the uprising, Las Casas vividly describes horrific massacres in which Spanish soldiers murdered scores of Indian men, women, and children, sometimes wiping out entire villages. The Spanish were deliberately cruel in their second war against the natives of Higüey, according to Las Casas, because they wanted to instill such terror in the Tainos that they would not even contemplate defying their Spanish rulers again. By the end of 1504, the brief but bloody uprising was over and the rebels' leader, Cotubanama, had been captured and imprisoned in Santo Domingo where he would soon be executed by order of the governor.

Ponce de León, according to Gonzalo Fernández de Oviedo, was an excellent fighter and military strategist—"a man spirited, sagacious and diligent in all warlike matters." His performance as captain of the Santo Domingo forces in the second Taino uprising must have been outstanding because soon after the Spaniards defeated the Indians in late 1504, Governor Ovando rewarded Ponce for his efforts by making him adelantado (frontier governor) of the province of Higüey. The office of adelantado had first developed during the Reconquest of the Iberian Peninsula from the Moors as a means of holding land won by the Catholic armies. The position of adelantado would be used frequently by the Spaniards in their colonization of the Caribbean islands and South and Central America as a means of protecting and maintaining order in territories acquired from the Indians.

To help distribute the Spanish population on Hispaniola and better regulate native population centers in the wake of the Taino uprising, along with making Ponce adelantado of Higüey, Governor Ovando authorized the creation of two new Spanish pueblos (towns) in the province in early 1505. One pueblo was to be built near the sea, the other some miles inland. Ovando, who evidently had great faith in Ponce's administrative and military abilities, appointed Juan as his deputy and captain in the pueblo closest to the shoreline. In addition, he gave his young protégé the honor of naming the new town. Ponce called it

Salvaleón, presumably in honor of the Castilian estate where his aristocratic maternal grandmother had grown up.

For his assistance in putting down the rebellion in Higüey, Ponce was also rewarded by his appreciative governor with an encomienda, a grant of land that typically included an Indian village or cluster of villages, and a repartimiento, a set number of Indians to be used for forced labor. According to Anthony Devereux, a typical repartimiento of early sixteenth-century Hispaniola would have consisted of between 30 and 80 Indians. Ponce may have received as many as 100 Indian laborers as part of his repartimiento, however, because of his status as an official of the crown.

By order of Ferdinand and Isabella, only warring Indians could be legally enslaved in Hispaniola. Yet the Indian workers of the repartimiento/encomienda system were slaves in everything but name, for they could be moved wherever the Spanish

THE TAINO

Thought to be descended from the Arawak people of Venezuela, the Taino were the largest Indian group in the Caribbean in the late fifteenth and early sixteenth centuries. They resided not only on Hispaniola, but also on Puerto Rico, Cuba, and Jamaica as well as on many smaller islands in the Caribbean basin. The Taino, who clustered together into small villages, constructed their houses from the trunks and fronds of palm trees. They were fishermen, small game hunters, gatherers, and farmers, growing yucca, sweet potatoes, beans, peanuts, and squash in fields of easy-to-tend mounds. They exhibited great creativity in weaving, woodwork, ceramics, sculpture, music, poetry, and dance. Today, Taino culture lives on not only in the traditional dances, songs, crafts, and cuisine of the Caribbean islands, but also in the many words Spanish and English-speaking peoples borrowed from their language over the years including barbecue, hammock, canoe, tobacco, and manatee (a large sea mammal).

grantee—or encomendero—chose and made to toil at whatever he desired, most often mining or farming. Indeed, New World encomendero often spoke of "owning" the Indian men, women, and children who had been commended (granted) to them. In theory, the Indians entrusted to an encomendero were supposed to receive adequate housing, food, and daily wages as well as instruction in Roman Catholic doctrine in exchange for their labor. In actual practice, most Indians probably received few if any of these things, for colonial authorities made no effort to monitor the system.

The encomienda/repartimiento system in which Juan Ponce took part in Hispaniola was not a completely novel arrangement to the Castilians who colonized the New World. Rather, it was reminiscent of the system long used by the Castilian crown to repopulate and protect areas taken from the Moors during the Reconquista, in which knights were compensated for their military service with land and other spoils of war. In essence, the institutions of encomiendo and repartimiento were a means for the royal government to both reward their loyal Spanish servants in the New World and to settle, defend, and make a profit from newly acquired territories.

With the indispensable assistance of the Indians who were commended to him, Juan Ponce turned his grant of fertile land along Higüey's Yuma River into a highly productive plantation, growing cassava for bread, sweet potatoes—another staple of both the Indians' and the colonists' diets—and a variety of other vegetables as well as cattle, pigs, and horses. Soon he was supplying the Spanish ships that regularly left the port of Santo Domingo to the west of Salvaleón for Europe. At the nearby Bay of Yuma, cassava bread and other products from Ponce's farm were loaded onto the ships as last minute provisions before the vessels headed for the open Atlantic.

Because of its strategic location along the water route from Hispaniola's main port at Santo Domingo to the Atlantic Ocean, Juan Ponce's farm made him a wealthy man, allowing him to live in style in Salvaleón. Not content to settle for a mud-walled, thatched roof cottage such as most early Spanish colonists lived in, Ponce had his Indian laborers build him a spacious stone house in Salvaleón. Ponce shared his new home with his family—his wife Leonor and their four children, three daughters—Juana, María and Isabel—and one son, Luis.

Little is known about Leonor except that she came from Castile originally and was living in Santo Domingo with her innkeeper father when Ponce courted and married her sometime after returning to Hispaniola in the spring of 1502. She could not have resided in Hispaniola for more than three or four years at the time she met Ponce, for the first female Spanish colonists arrived on the island in 1498 with Columbus' third expedition across the Atlantic. On his third voyage, Columbus was permitted by royal decree to bring one female to Hispaniola for every 10 immigrants. On his previous voyages, he had been forbidden to include any women among his passengers, which is surprising considering that the colonization of Hispaniola was supposed to be a central goal of his second expedition in 1493.

By 1506, Ponce de León was one of Hispaniola's leading citizens. Not only was he a frontier governor and a military captain, he was also a wealthy landowner, a husband and a father. Yet Ponce was not satisfied. Possessed of a restless spirit, he always seemed to be in search of a new challenge, a novel opportunity. As it turned out, he would find his next adventure just 70 miles away from his home at Salvaleón on a lushly beautiful island the Tainos called Borinquén and which we know today as Puerto Rico.

5

Conquering Puerto Rico

We have no way of knowing what Juan Ponce de León was thinking on November 19, 1493 when he first saw the island of Borinquén— or San Juan Bautista—as Christopher Columbus dubbed the new land during his second transatlantic expedition. But perhaps even then, more than a decade before he would lead the Castilian conquest and settlement of Puerto Rico, Ponce dreamed of one day staking his claim to the island's fertile valleys, palm-fringed beaches, and lush hills.

Although struck by the beauty of the island, Christopher Columbus never returned to San Juan Bautista. Indeed, for a dozen years after the admiral claimed the island for Ferdinand and Isabella, Spanish colonists and officials alike all but ignored Borinquén, except to use it now and then as a convenient place for their ships to obtain fresh water before heading for the open Atlantic and Europe. During the early years of Spanish empire building in the New World, the new settlers were preoccupied with conquering, colonizing, and hunting for gold and other precious commodities on Puerto Rico's much

Costa Isabella, named for the Spanish queen who funded Columbus' expeditions to the West, is part of Puerto Rico's majestic landscape. Though rich in plant and mineral resources and home to an excellent natural harbor, Puerto Rico (then called Borinquén or San Juan Bautista) was largely overlooked by Spanish colonists until the 1500s. Ponce de León would eventually be named the island's governor.

larger neighbor to the west—Hispaniola. (At about 3,500 square miles, Puerto Rico is the fourth biggest island in the Caribbean Sea compared to Cuba at approximately 44,200 square miles, Hispaniola at 29,400, and Jamaica at 4,400 square miles.) In April 1505, Vicente Yañez Pinzón, a pilot on Columbus' first voyage, was actually given a royal patent to settle Puerto Rico in appreciation for his services to the crown. In a symbolic gesture, Pinzón announced his intention to colonize (San Juan Bautista) Borinquén by shipping a herd of goats and sheep to the island from Hispaniola. Yet Pinzón never got around to sending even one human settler to Puerto Rico or to constructing a fortress there, as stipulated in his contract with King Ferdinand (Queen Isabella had died in 1504). Consequently, in April 1506, 12 months after his royal license was granted, Pinzón's rights to colonize and govern the island were revoked.

Pinzón evidently placed little value on the patent he had been awarded for colonizing Puerto Rico. Back in Salvaleón, however, Juan Ponce de León had developed a profound interest in the island that lay so near his seaside home. At the root of the adelantado's fascination with Puerto Rico were reports he had heard about the island from local Indians. During the first years of the sixteenth century, an estimated 30,000-50,000 Taino lived on Borinquén. The Taino people of Higüey traded frequently with them, paddling back and forth across the narrow Mona Passage separating their homeland from Borinquén in dugout canoes. According to Gonzalo Fernández de Oviedo, several Indians who paid regular visits to Puerto Rico informed Ponce that there was gold for the taking on Borinquén, showing him a few nuggets of the precious metal as proof. Although Ponce's agricultural pursuits in eastern Hispaniola were making him a wealthy man, he was still tempted by the prospect of finding a significant new source of gold. Ponce was probably also entranced by the promise of a new adventure and the prestige he would surely gain in Hispaniola as well as the royal court should he successfully conquer and exploit this rich, unexplored territory for the empire.

After learning of Puerto Rico's alleged mineral wealth from his Taino informants, Ponce conveyed the thrilling news to his mentor, Governor Ovando, according to Oviedo. Although Oviedo's chronicle and other traditional accounts place Ponce's first voyage to Puerto Rico in August of 1508, many modern scholars, including Robert Fuson and the respected Puerto Rican historian Aurelio Tió, now believe that Ponce made a secret exploratory expedition to the island at Ovando's behest two years earlier, in the summer of 1506.

Much of the evidence for Ponce's clandestine journey of 1506 rests on a document prepared in Mexico in 1532 regarding the achievements and merits of Ponce's cousin, Juan González Ponce de León. In the document, Juan González testified that one of his most important services to the crown over the past two decades was to accompany Ponce and about 200 other men from Santo Domingo, Hispaniola to Puerto Rico in June 1506. The five-ship fleet, which had been authorized by Governor Ovando and was under Ponce's command, arrived at Puerto Rico's western coast on June 24, according to Juan González.

Soon after going ashore, Captain Ponce was greeted by a group of friendly Taino Indians, Juan González testified. The commander relied on his cousin, who was fluent in the Indians' language, to act as his interpreter. With Juan González's help, Juan Ponce learned from the Indians about an excellent natural harbor on the island's northeastern coast. The captain assigned his cousin to command a small scouting party composed of Spaniards and Taino guides to travel to the bay. As they hiked across the island's interior, Juan González and his men searched for gold. To their delight, they found a number of large nuggets in the streams and rivers they passed along their way. Finally, they arrived at the harbor, which turned out to be exceptionally deep and well sheltered from winds. After making his way back to Ponce's encampment on the island's western coast, Juan González gave his cousin a glowing report of the harbor (which would eventually become known as San Juan Bay) and of Puerto Rico's mineral riches.

Impressed by the amount and quality of the gold gathered by the men on their journey eastward and hoping to locate more of the valuable metal, Juan Ponce decided to send his five ships with skeleton crews to San Juan Bay while he and the rest of his company marched over land to the harbor, collecting gold nuggets along the way. On glimpsing the fine bay at San Juan, Captain

Ponce decided he had found the perfect spot to build Puerto Rico's first Spanish settlement. Construction on the village, eventually named Caparra, probably began in late 1506 or early 1507, Fuson believes, with the erection of several huts fashioned from thatch and cane. Located on a hill above a mosquito-filled swamp, the town of Caparra would be moved to a more accessible and healthier location further north along the harbor in 1521 and renamed Puerto Rico (Rich Port). Soon after, the names of the port city and the island were switched, so that the city was called San Juan and the island was called Puerto Rico.

Sometime during the winter of 1507, Juan Ponce and his company of men returned to Hispaniola. Ponce promptly reported to Ovando regarding his expedition, presenting the governor with a large purse of gold collected from Puerto Rico's streams and rivers. No official report of the voyage was ever written up, however. Indeed, there is reason to believe that both Ponce and Ovando went to great pains to keep news of the expedition to Puerto Rico from seeping out. But why all the secrecy surrounding Ponce's trip of 1506?

Ponce and Ovando's chief reason for keeping the expedition a secret was almost certainly rooted in the political uncertainty then gripping Iberia's richest and most powerful kingdom, Castile. Following Isabella's death in 1504, the Castilian crown passed not to her husband Ferdinand but to her daughter, Juana, otherwise known as La Loca ("the crazy one"). Because of the grave doubts regarding Juana's mental competence, she was queen of Castile in name only, with her husband Felipe actually holding the reigns of power. When Felipe died unexpectedly in 1506, Castile was effectively left without a ruler until 1507 when Ferdinand was finally summoned from Aragon to act as regent for his troubled daughter.

In 1506, with the political situation in Castile still in turmoil, Ovando and Ponce probably thought it prudent to keep their expedition to Puerto Rico under wraps. Once Ferdinand reclaimed the throne of Castile in 1507 and the kingdom again achieved some degree of stability, however, the governor and his

After a period of instability in Castile, King Ferdinand (depicted in this portrait) was summoned from Aragon to restore order. Hearing of Ponce's claims of rich gold deposits on Puerto Rico, Ferdinand was eager to lay claim to the island's mineral reserves.

protégé confided in the king regarding what Ponce had found in Puerto Rico. No doubt they emphasized the region's fertile valleys, accommodating natives, and above all, rich gold deposits. The king was clearly impressed. On June 15, 1508, Ferdinand officially gave his permission to Juan Ponce de León to lead an expedition to San Juan Bautista for Castile. This accord between Ponce and the crown, Fuson believes, was arrived at primarily on the basis of the gold reserves which Ponce assured Ferdinand existed on the island.

In August 1508, Ponce set out from Higüey on what was actually his second journey to Puerto Rico, but his first official one. This new expedition was much smaller than the initial voyage, including just one ship and 50 men, as compared to five ships and perhaps four times as many sailors and soldiers in 1506. The historian Anthony Devereux speculates that Ovando sent a large expedition to Puerto Rico the first time around because he was uncertain of how the islanders would respond to the Spanish explorers and he hoped to intimidate them into submission. Since Ponce had found the islanders friendly and cooperative on his trip of 1506, he probably figured that a smaller party of men would suffice for his follow-up voyage. Because Ponce himself, and not the government of Hispaniola, was paying for the expedition this time, he may also have been hesitant to assume the costs of paying, feeding, and outfitting a bigger group.

Ponce and his men arrived on the southern coast of Puerto Rico on August 12, 1508 near the village of the island's supreme cacique, Agüeybaná. Ponce promised Agüeybaná that his soldiers would protect the Taino from another Caribbean tribe, the Caribs, if the cacique would order his subjects to assist the Spaniards in their construction, farming, and mining endeavors on Borinquén. The Caribs, a warlike and cannibalistic tribe, had been launching periodic attacks on Borinquén from the Virgin Islands and other islands to the east and south for years.

Agüeybaná readily agreed to Ponce's demand for Indian workers. Yet it is impossible to know whether the cacique cooperated with Ponce because of his pledge of protection against the bloodthirsty Caribs or because the cacique had heard reports from Hispaniola's Taino natives regarding the brutality of the Spaniards and was consequently afraid to stand up to the intruders.

After obtaining a large group of native laborers from Agüeybaná, Ponce sailed around the island to San Juan Bay and the site of the village he had founded some 18 months earlier. On arriving in Caparra, Ponce ordered some of the Indians to construct a big building with thick mud walls to serve as a fortress, barracks, and warehouse for the Spaniards. While another group of Indian laborers cleared farm fields and planted cassava for bread so the new settlers would not go hungry, Ponce had his men fan out from the village to prospect and mine for gold.

By 1509, having proved to the king that significant gold deposits did indeed exist on the island, Ponce successfully renegotiated his contract with the royal government, gaining permission to start colonizing San Juan Bautista in earnest. King Ferdinand also appointed Ponce as the island's first governor. Now that he was officially in charge, Ponce oversaw the division of Puerto Rico's land and Indians amongst the settlers according to the repartimiento/encomienda system used on Hispaniola. With his own large apportionment of Indian laborers, Ponce made his new plantation near Caparra a major supplier of cassava bread for the island's Spanish colonists and constructed a large house for himself and his family similar to the one they owned in Salvaleón.

Governor Ponce proved an energetic and competent administrator. In contrast to Christopher Columbus' earlier administration of Hispaniola, Ponce ran Puerto Rico's economic and political affairs efficiently, handling the colonists with firmness yet also with tact. According to his contemporaries and most historians, Governor Ponce was universally respected by the Spaniards who served under him for his scrupulous honesty and fairness.

Just how fairly Ponce treated the native peoples of Puerto Rico is a matter for debate, however. Ponce, Bartolomé de las Casas accuses in his history of the New World, built up his wealth and influence in San Juan Bautista not by his own efforts or abilities but "on the labors, blood and sufferings of his [Indian] subjects." In marked contrast to Las Casas, other historians including both of Ponce's chief American biographers, Devereux and Fuson, assert that Ponce's treatment of the Indians was mild and benevolent compared to that of other Spanish officials and conquistadors of the era. In support of his view regarding Ponce's good relations with the Indians, Devereux quotes the eighteenth-century Spanish historian Iñigo Abbad y Lasierra who claimed

Ponce de León proved a capable governor of Puerto Rico, ruling colonists with a strict but reputedly even hand. The quality of his treatment of the local Indians, however, remains debatable. Ponce's quelling of a Taino uprising was reported to be both ruthless and efficient.

that Juan Ponce de León "by his prudent conduct and humanity won the confidence and love of the Indians."

It would appear, however, that the governor failed to win "the confidence and love" of all the Indians of Puerto Rico, for in early 1511, a Taino uprising erupted in the western part of the island and from there spread rapidly throughout the rest of Borinquén. For some time, the Taino had been disgruntled by the exploitative intruders who had originally presented themselves as the natives' "protectors" from their old enemies, the Caribs. Perpetually exhausted and hungry, they were fed up with the Spaniards' burdensome demands for tribute and labor. With the death of their supreme cacique Agüeybaná, whose policy had been to placate the invaders, the Taino determined to rebel against their abusive overlords. One of the chief rebel leaders was the deceased Agüeybaná's namesake and son (some accounts say his nephew), Agüeybaná II. After Agüeybaná II directed his warriors to launch raids against isolated Spanish towns, first in western Borinquén and then in other parts of the island, Governor Ponce quickly raised an army to hunt down and punish the insurgents.

A notorious participant in the 1511 war between the Taino and the Spaniards was the Governor's fierce war dog, Becerrillo (Little Bull). According to Oviedo, Becerrillo was "of red pelt and black eyes, medium sized and not bad looking." Like the other vicious dogs used by Spanish troops to control the native peoples of their New World colonies, Becerrillo was trained to search out and disable runaway Indians as well as to kill Indian warriors in battle. According to Oviedo, Becerrillo was so skilled at tracking down and terrorizing Indians that he was worth 50 soldiers to Ponce in his campaign to subdue the Taino. Ponce was said to have fed his valuable mascot the same rations he gave his troops and even to have paid him the same wages. Oviedo reports that Ponce generously presented Becerrillo's pup, Leoncillo (Little Lion), to his close friend and fellow conquistador, Vasco Núñez de Balboa. Leoncillo, who like his father was known for his ferocity and courage in battle, was reportedly with Balboa when he marched across the Isthmus of Panama and discovered the Pacific Ocean for Castile in 1513.

With the assistance of attack dogs like Becerrillo and their vastly superior weapons, Ponce's army soon vanquished the much larger rebel forces. After their leader Agüeybaná II was killed in battle, many of the Taino warriors went into hiding in Borinquén's mountain ranges and dense forests or fled by canoe to nearby islands. By the spring of 1511, the native islanders' brief, desperate bid for freedom was over.

Yet, although he had succeeded in quelling the Taino rebellion by early 1511, as the year progressed, Ponce found himself facing grave political problems in his new island home. Ever since the death of Christopher Columbus in 1506 in Castile, a bitter legal struggle had been going on between the crown and Columbus' eldest son Diego that was rooted in Christopher Columbus' original contracts with Ferdinand and Isabella. When Columbus embarked on his first voyage of discovery for Ferdinand and Isabella in 1492, the Catholic monarchs had promised him the titles of viceroy and governor general over all lands he discovered. Columbus demanded that these titles be hereditary, meaning that upon his death they would automatically pass to his first born son, Diego, along with all other rights and privileges he held as a result of his agreements with the crown.

Even though Columbus' titles of viceroy and governor general had been stripped of any actual authority by 1500 as a

PUERTO RICO AFTER JUAN PONCE

Soon after Ponce left office, the island's new governor authorized the importation of African slaves to labor in Puerto Rico's mines and fields. By the time black slaves were introduced to Puerto Rico in 1513, the island's natives only numbered about 4,000 (as opposed to 30,000-50,000 before colonization). Although many Taino died or fled the island during the rebellion of 1511, most of the decrease in their numbers resulted from disease. Because they had no immunity to European illnesses, the Tainos died in droves from smallpox and other infections the Spaniards brought with them to the Caribbean. By the 1520s, Puerto Rico's gold supplies had been depleted and sugar cultivation had become its economic mainstay. In 1898 Puerto Rico became an U.S. territory following Spain's defeat in the Spanish-American War. In 1952 the Commonwealth of Puerto Rico was proclaimed, establishing the island as an autonomous part of the United States.

consequence of his unsatisfactory political performance on Hispaniola, his heir Diego insisted that not only the titles—but the political power that had originally been vested in them— were rightfully his. In the fall of 1509, despite the fact that his lawsuit against the crown had yet to be been decided, Diego was able to use his many political connections in Castile to obtain an appointment as interim or acting viceroy and governor general of the islands his father had discovered, including Hispaniola and San Juan Bautista. Although specifically commanded by the Spanish courts not to interfere with Ponce's government in Puerto Rico until his lawsuit was officially settled, Diego could not resist taking his revenge on Ponce, whom Diego disdained as the protégé of Nicolas de Ovando, the usurper of his father's position as governor of what was then Spain's premier New World colony, Hispaniola. Ordering Ponce to step aside, in October 1509 Diego assigned his associate Juan Cerón to serve as chief administrator of the island and another crony, Miguel Díaz de Aux, to act as Puerto Rico's high sheriff.

By this time, however, Ponce had become something of a favorite of King Ferdinand, who seems to have had great faith in the conquistador's administrative abilities. In early 1510, Ferdinand sent a dispatch to San Juan Bautista repudiating the interim viceroy's actions in Puerto Rico and declaring Ponce de León to be the governor, captain, and chief justice of the island. For some reason, Ponce failed to receive the king's message until June of that year. Once he had the dispatch in hand, Ponce moved quickly, informing Cerón and Díaz that they would have to give up their posts at once. When the two men refused, Ponce had them arrested and shipped back to Castile in chains.

Ponce's reassertion of his authority over Puerto Rico was destined to be brief, however. In May 1511, the royal council of Castile finally made a ruling regarding the dispute between Diego Columbus and the crown. Diego was victorious—all of his father's political and financial rights and privileges regarding the New World islands he had discovered were to be permanently returned to his eldest son and heir. By November,

Derived from an ancient Spanish painting, the above picture depicts Christopher Columbus and his two sons Diego and Ferdinand. After the death of Christopher Columbus, Diego laid claim to his inheritance in the New World. After a long legal challenge, the crown eventually removed Ponce de León as governor of Puerto Rico, giving control to Columbus' son Diego.

the new viceroy had removed Ponce as governor of San Juan Bautista and reinstated his friend Cerón in his place. Diego Columbus and his associates in Puerto Rico, including the understandably bitter Cerón and Díaz, then set out to use every means at their disposal to harass the former governor.

Over the next year, Ponce's enemies in Puerto Rico kept him under continuous pressure, accusing him of financial improprieties, threatening to take away the Indians he had been awarded in encomienda/repartimiento to labor in his fields and mines, and even confiscating his ship for a time so that he became a virtual prisoner on the island. As difficult as Ponce's situation in Puerto Rico may have been, however, he did have one important friend looking out for him—King Ferdinand. Ferdinand made sure that Ponce retained his position as military captain of the island and wrote to Ponce on more than one occasion to assure him of his support. "As for you . . . come to see me so as to inform me of affairs over there and what you may wish to undertake so that I may make arrangements to help in whichever way I can," he wrote to Juan Ponce early in the summer of 1511.

In July 1511, King Ferdinand ordered his royal commissioner in Santo Domingo, Miguel de Pasamonte, to approach Ponce with a bold new adventure—one that would involve leaving Puerto Rico to explore and claim new territory for the crown, territory that would not fall under Diego Columbus' jurisdiction. For some time, Ferdinand had been aware of unexplored lands to the north of Hispaniola and Cuba, and particularly of a large island popularly known as Bimini (also spelled Beimini, Benimy, or Bimene). Following Ferdinand's directions, Pasamonte strongly urged Ponce to prepare a formal proposal to the crown for an expedition to the uncharted island.

With Diego and his cohorts clearly determined to make life difficult for him on Puerto Rico, Ponce jumped at Pasamonte's offer. With the royal commissioner's assistance, he drew up a plan for exploring and settling the island. Although Ponce's was not the only proposal regarding Bimini submitted to the king in 1511—Christopher Columbus' brother Bartholomew also submitted a contract to find and conquer the island—Ponce's plan was the one the crown chose to support. The groundwork had been laid for Ponce to embark on the most important adventure of his career.

6

The Quest
for Bimini

On February 23, 1512, a formal agreement between the crown
and Juan Ponce de León for the exploration and settlement of
Bimini was signed by Ferdinand and dispatched to Puerto Rico.
Ferdinand told Ponce the contract was a reward for his many
services to the crown and evidence of the profound confidence he
retained in the former governor. "When you find and discover the
said Island," the royal contract stated, "I grant to you the government and justice of it for all of the days of your life." To "show greater
benefit and favor to you," the patent continued, "it is my will and
pleasure that you shall have the government and settlement of all
the islands in the neighborhood of the said Island of Benimy
(Bimini), if you should personally discover them." For a period of
12 years after his discovery of Bimini and any nearby islands,
Ferdinand pledged, Ponce would receive "a tenth of all the revenues
and profits" gleaned from the "gold, and other metals and profitable

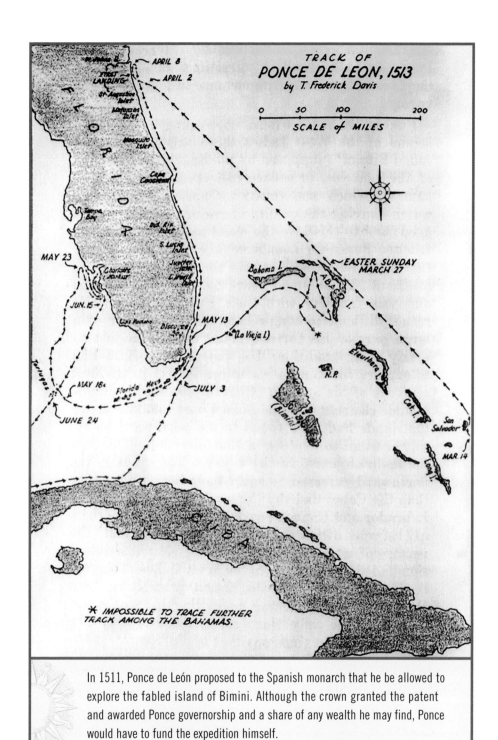

TRACK OF
PONCE DE LEON, 1513
by T. Frederick Davis

SCALE of MILES

EASTER SUNDAY
MARCH 27

* IMPOSSIBLE TO TRACE FURTHER
TRACK AMONG THE BAHAMAS.

In 1511, Ponce de León proposed to the Spanish monarch that he be allowed to explore the fabled island of Bimini. Although the crown granted the patent and awarded Ponce governorship and a share of any wealth he may find, Ponce would have to fund the expedition himself.

things" which the king anticipated would be found in the new territories. Ponce, however, would have to foot the entire bill for the expedition himself.

Historians have long debated why Ponce and Ferdinand were interested in finding Bimini in the first place. The traditional story associated with Ponce's quest for Bimini is that he believed the island was the site of a fountain of youth capable of restoring vigor—and particularly sexual vigor—to men past their prime. However, not a single word is said about locating a magical fountain in Ponce's royal patent of February 1512. Indeed, the entire story about Ponce and the rejuvenating fountain comes not from primary sources such as official documents or private letters or journals, but from a secondary source written years after the expedition took place: Antonio de Herrera y Tordesillas' 1601 chronicle of early Spanish America, *Historia general.* Herrera, in turn, apparently based his account of the youth-restoring fountain on a history of the New World published in 1516 by the Italian-born scholar and cleric Peter Martyr, who became the Americas' first chronicler, although he never set foot in the New World himself.

According to Martyr, the native peoples of Puerto Rico, Hispaniola, and Cuba were convinced that a rejuvenating fountain existed somewhere to the north of their homelands, on the mysterious island of Bimini. On Bimini, the Indians insisted, was "a spring of running water of such marvelous virtue, that the water thereof being drunk . . . makes old men young again," wrote Martyr. For his history of Spanish America, Herrera borrowed Martyr's rendition of the fountain myth. Unlike Martyr, however, Herrera directly linked the Indian legend to Ponce's expedition in search of Bimini. Although Herrera states that Ponce's chief motivations for his voyage were "to enhance his self-esteem and to augment his estate," he claims that Ponce was also inspired by the intriguing tales he had heard about Bimini, and "especially that singular Fuente (fountain or spring) that the Indians spoke of, that turned men from old men to boys."

Fuson and Devereux agree that Ponce would have been aware of the widely circulated native tales regarding a fountain of youth and the close association of the magical fuente with Bimini. Both historians also agree, however, that looking for the fountain was not a primary motivation for Ponce in his exploratory voyage. Rather, the two scholars contend, with his political career in Puerto Rico destroyed, Ponce was concerned above all with finding new territories to exploit and govern. Devereux furthermore argues that if anyone associated with the expedition had incentive for wanting to find a fountain of youth, it was Ferdinand, and not Ponce, who was only 38 years old in 1512 (assuming a birth date of 1474). Following Queen Isabella's death in 1504, Ferdinand married Germaine de Foix, a French woman many years his junior. In 1512, when the king sanctioned Ponce's voyage to Bimini, Germaine was 25 and Ferdinand 60 years old. Devereux suggests that Ferdinand, who never sired a child with his youthful second wife, may well have had his reasons for wanting Ponce to locate the fountain that made old men young again.

Fuson, however, dismisses the importance of the fountain even for Ferdinand. Ferdinand "felt a strong moral obligation to repay Juan Ponce for many years of service and loyalty," Fuson contends, and was, moreover, "casting about for a sound investment" when he authorized Ponce's expedition to Bimini. "At best," he concludes, as far as both Ferdinand and Ponce were concerned, "the quest for the magic fountain was a secondary motive for the exploration, and most likely it was a tertiary one."

It would take a full year for Ponce to obtain the sailing vessels, provisions, and crews required for the voyage to Bimini approved by Ferdinand in February 1512. On March 4, 1513, Ponce finally set sail from Puerto Rico with three ships, 65 passengers, including two free African sailors, two

Indian slaves, two women (the wife and the sister of one of the crew members), several cattle, and his horse. Sailing along the outer edge of the Bahamas, the fleet called at San Salvador, Columbus' first American landfall, then headed northwestward. On the morning of April 3, the voyagers sighted what they believed to be a large island. Since the new land was discovered one week after Easter Sunday, Ponce named it La Florida (the flowered one) in honor of the Easter season which Spaniards commonly referred to as Pascua de Flores (Passover of Flowers). A landing party then went ashore and Ponce formally took possession of La Florida in the name of King Ferdinand.

The chief—and virtually the only—source for the 1513 expedition to Florida is Herrera, who published his *Historia general* nearly 90 years after Ponce's expedition. Supposedly, Herrera had access to the original log of the voyage, which was subsequently lost. Unfortunately, Herrera's description of the 230-day voyage contains many significant gaps. His account, for example, does not tell us where Ponce first landed in Florida, except that it was someplace on the eastern or Atlantic Coast. Although some scholars believe that Ponce landed near the site of the Spanish town of St. Augustine, which would be founded approximately 50 years later, other researchers are convinced that Ponce landed farther south along the Florida coastline. Fuson thinks Ponce probably touched land on an uninhabited stretch of seashore a few miles north of modern-day Daytona Beach.

According to Herrera's account, after spending a few days exploring on shore, Ponce and his fleet headed northward briefly, then turned southward, sailing along the peninsula's eastern coast to the vicinity of present-day West Palm Beach. There Ponce and his chief pilot, Antón de Alaminos, made one of the most important discoveries of the entire voyage: the powerful current we know today as the Gulf Stream. In Herrera's words, the fleet "encountered a current that they were unable to sail

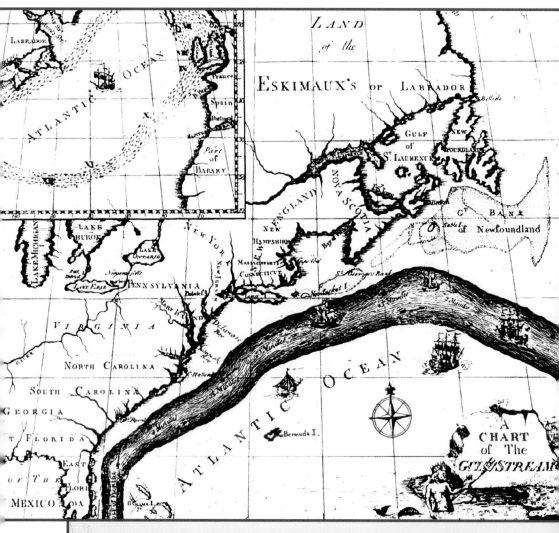

This eighteenth-century map charts the Gulf Stream, a fast-moving current within the Atlantic Ocean, which Ponce and his chief pilot discovered on their Florida expedition. The current soon became immensely important to the Spanish, who used the swift route to transport gold and riches they acquired in the Americas back to Spain.

against even though they had a strong wind. They not only could not move forward but [moved] backward although they seemed to be sailing well. Finally they realized that the current was stronger than the wind." A fast-moving current in the ocean, the Gulf Stream flows out of the Caribbean Sea into the Gulf of Mexico and through the narrow Straits of Florida, then shoots northward up Florida's Atlantic Coast before heading out to sea around Cape Hatteras, North Carolina. Eventually, the stream ends up off the coast of Norway in the North Atlantic, thousands of miles from Florida. Ponce and Alaminos' discovery of the Gulf Stream would prove immensely important for the development of Spain's New World empire. Following Ponce's voyage, Spanish navigators hit upon the idea of using the Gulf Stream, which moves at speeds up to five miles per hour, as their swiftest route back across the Atlantic. After Spain conquered Mexico and Peru in the 1520s, this new and quicker route eastward became particularly valuable to the crown as treasure fleets carrying gold and other riches from the former Aztec and Inca empires relied on the current as their oceanic expressway home.

Soon after discovering the Gulf Stream, Ponce had his first encounter with the native peoples of Florida when he decided to go ashore with a small landing party. On the beach, the Spaniards were approached by a group of Indians who attempted to seize their longboat and weapons. Ponce tried to avoid an altercation but after "the Indians hit a sailor in the head with a stick, knocking him unconscious, he had to fight with them. The Indians, with their arrows and spears, with points made from sharpened bone or fish spines, wounded two Castilians," Herrera reports. A shaken Juan Ponce then "collected his men, with some difficulty, and they departed during the night," according to Herrera.

Following his skirmish with the Indians, Ponce continued sailing southward until he reached the tip of Florida. Not understanding Florida's peninsular nature and still convinced that the large land mass he had discovered was an island, he attempted to round it, sailing westward through the string of small islands known today as the Florida Keys, then veering northward up Florida's Gulf (or western) Coast. Most scholars believe that

Ponce sailed as far north as Charlotte Harbor, between the modern-day cities of Sarasota and Fort Myers.

On the Gulf Coast, Ponce entered the domain of the warlike Calusa Indians. After his fleet anchored at one of the barrier islands near Charlotte Harbor and Fort Myers—possibly modern-day Pine Island—a group of Calusa paddled out to the ships in dugout canoes and tried to haul in one of the vessels "by pulling the anchor cable by hand," according to Herrera. Ponce responded by sending a longboat after the warriors. Upon reaching land, the boat's crew took four Calusa women hostage and smashed two Indian canoes.

For the next several weeks, Ponce's fleet remained in the area. Herrera indicates that the Spaniards stayed on because the four Indian hostages told them that their cacique, Chief Carlos, had gold and might be willing to trade with the foreigners. Eventually, an Indian who understood Spanish (probably a native of Hispaniola or one of the other islands colonized by the Spaniards) approached the anchored sailing vessels in a canoe. The cacique would soon paddle out to Ponce to trade gold with him, the Indian promised. This story, however, turned out to be a ruse. Instead of being greeted by Chief Carlos, Ponce and his men were confronted by a fleet of 80 canoes filled with Calusa warriors shooting arrows at them. The Calusa finally withdrew in defeat when it became clear their arrows were no match for the Spaniards' guns and crossbows.

Soon after his battle with the Calusa, Ponce decided to conclude the expedition and head back for Puerto Rico, which he had departed nearly four months earlier. On his way home, Ponce stopped at a small cluster of islands about 70 miles west of Florida that his Indian hostages had told him about. He named the islands Las Tortugas (later known as the Dry Tortugas because they contained no fresh water source) for the 160 giant tortugas (turtles) his men captured and killed there during a single evening. From Las Tortugas, Ponce headed homeward by way of Cuba, the Florida Keys, and the Bahamas.

In the Bahamas, Ponce ordered his best pilot, Antón de Alaminos, to take a ship, two Indian guides, and the necessary crew to look for the elusive island of Bimini and, if Herrera is believed, the magic fountain one last time. While Ponce and his crew made their way back to Puerto Rico, arriving there in October 1513, Alaminos combed the Bahamas island chain. In February 1514, he returned home with the news that he had found Bimini (probably modern-day Andros Island). According to Herrera, Almaninos informed Ponce that the island had plenty of lakes but no miraculous rejuvenating spring.

Most historians link Ponce's decision to terminate his 1513 expedition to the violent clash between his forces and the Calusa on Florida's Gulf Coast. Some of these scholars have suggested a startling reason for the intense hostility with which the Calusa greeted Ponce and his men in 1513. By the time Ponce encountered them, these historians contend, the Calusa had already formed an extremely low opinion of the Spaniards based on their prior experiences with Spanish slavers. Robert Fuson is among those scholars who believes

THE CALUSA

A confederation of tribes, the Calusa inhabited the coastal region of southwestern Florida and the small outlying islands at the time of Ponce's voyages to the region. The Calusa lived primarily by hunting, fishing, and gathering berries and nuts. Although less dependent on agriculture for their food than the Taino, they raised squash and a few other crops. A warlike people in terms of both military power and political influence, the Calusa were the single most important native group in southern Florida in the early sixteenth century. By the late eighteenth century, the Calusa had completely disappeared from Florida, most of them victims of smallpox and other diseases which the Spanish and other European colonists and explorers unwittingly brought with them to the Calusas' homeland.

that at least one unauthorized Spanish slaving expedition visited Florida before Ponce de León ever set foot on the peninsula. Since the late 1490s, Spanish slave hunters had been raiding the Bahamas as the native population of Hispaniola steadily declined due to overwork, starvation, and above all, the introduction of European diseases. By 1510 the Bahamas' indigenous population, which had originally numbered some 10,000 Taino, had been almost entirely decimated (destroyed) by the slavers. Yet, the need for Indian labor in the mines and farm fields of Hispaniola as well as in Puerto Rico and Cuba, where the Indian populations had also been gravely depleted by the early sixteenth century, was greater than ever. Therefore, contends Fuson, "it is only logical to believe that slavers sought their prey in Florida after the neighboring islands had been emptied."

In support of his theory that slavers visited Florida before Ponce landed there in 1513, Fuson cites Bartolomé de las Casas' *Historia de las indias* (*History of the Indies*). According to Las Casas, in early 1511 in Santo Domingo, Hispaniola "a group came together and fitted out several ships in order to go out and capture the innocent people [Indians] who lived on the small islands [Bahamas]." Las Casas writes:

> [After reaching the Bahamas, the slavers] searched many of them very thoroughly, but found nothing . . . and because it seemed to them that they were going to return empty-handed, not only losing the money that had been invested . . . but facing the embarrassment of returning to this island [Hispaniola] without extracting some profit from their voyage, they decided to go toward the north to discover land, as long as the provisions held out, and they found it. . . . It is certain that this was the land and coastline that now we call Florida. . . . They returned to Santo Domingo with their prize [a cargo of Indian slaves].

Since the 1511 expedition, and any other slaving voyages to Florida that may have taken place before 1513, were not sanctioned by the royal government, it seems probable that Ponce would not have known about them and thus sincerely believed that he was the first Spaniard to reach Florida. Even if Ponce had been aware of any earlier slaving expeditions to the peninsula, his was the first authorized voyage of exploration to Bimini and Florida. Consequently, on returning home to Puerto Rico, Ponce promptly petitioned the crown for permission to make a second voyage to the lands he had "discovered" for Spain.

In early 1514, Ponce decided to strengthen his petition by taking his request directly to King Ferdinand in Castile. At the royal court, Ponce presented his sovereign with 5,000 gold pesos (Spanish currency) from Puerto Rican mines—a considerable sum. Undoubtedly, Ferdinand appreciated the tribute, but he also seems to have been favorably impressed by Ponce de León himself, who reputedly possessed a great deal of personal charm. In his long narrative poem about the early conquistadors, the Spanish poet-historian Juan de Castellanos characterized Ponce as amiable and attractive:

> He was somewhat of ruddy hue, with a pleasing face,
> Affable and well loved by his people,
> Well put together in all proportions . . .

Castellanos, a younger contemporary of Ponce, may have been personally acquainted with Ponce in Spain. He may also have obtained his information on Ponce's appearance and disposition from his fellow historian Oviedo, who provided Castellanos with anecdotes about other early conquistadors with whom he was acquainted in the New World and in Spain.

For whatever reason—Ponce's generous gift of gold, his personal charm, or his many services to the crown as explorer, soldier, and government official—Ferdinand decided to bestow on Ponce an honor never before received by a conquistador by knighting him and presenting him with his own coat-of-arms. Henceforth, Ponce would be known as Don (Sir) Juan Ponce de León. Additionally, Ferdinand awarded Ponce with the contract he had requested for a second voyage to explore and colonize Florida and Bimini and named him governor and chief justice of the lands he discovered.

A novel feature of Ponce's second patent with the crown was that it commanded the conquistador to inform all Indians inhabiting the lands he discovered of "El Requerimiento" (The Requirement). First developed by church officials in 1513, the Requerimiento was a lengthy document describing the central tenets of the Christian faith and proclaiming the supremacy of the Catholic pope. Spanish explorers were required to read the Requerimiento to any Indians they encountered on their voyages before they could use force against the natives. The Requerimiento concluded by ordering its Indian listeners to accept the Christian message and submit to the pope and their new Spanish rulers. Typically recited to the Indians in Spanish or Latin, the reading of the document "was usually met with blank stares—interpreted as rejection," notes the historian Zvi Dor-Ner. Once the Requerimiento had been presented to the Indians, assuming they "rejected" its commands (which was almost always the case, although most Indians probably hadn't the slightest idea of what they were spurning), the Spanish forces were then legally authorized by their government and church to attack and kill or enslave the "heathens" who had scorned the efforts to convert them.

Although Ponce's royal patent to explore and settle Florida and Bimini was awarded on September 27, 1514, seven years were to pass before the return voyage took place. One of the chief reasons for this delay was a rash of attacks by the Caribs on Spanish settlements in the Caribbean. While Ponce was still gone on his 1513 voyage of exploration, Carib warriors, probably from the Virgin Islands, raided Caparra, where Ponce and his family made their home in Puerto Rico, destroying Ponce's house and most of the town. Determined to punish the Caribs, Ponce asked Ferdinand for permission to lead an armada against them before embarking on his second expedition to Florida. Ferdinand readily granted Ponce's request, lending him a fleet of three vessels. By May 1515, Ponce and his small armada were

THE REQUERIMIENTO

The following passage is excerpted from The Requerimiento, *or* The Requirement, *a document that Spanish explorers were required to read to the Indians they encountered on their explorations. It asserted the supremacy of both the Spanish monarchs and the Catholic pope, and concluded by stating that if the Indians did not accept the terms outlined in the document, then extreme consequences, such as war, would result.*

On behalf of the king . . . and the queen . . . subjugators of barbarous peoples, we, their servants, notify and make known to you as best we are able, that God, Our Lord, living and eternal, created the heavens and the earth, and a man and a woman, of whom you and we and all other people of the world were, and are, the descendants. . . .

Of all these people God, Our Lord, chose one, who was called Saint Peter, to be the lord and the one who was to be superior to all the other people of the world, whom all should obey. . . . He was called the Pope. . . .

One of the past Popes who succeeded Saint Peter . . . as Lord of the Earth gave these islands and mainlands of the Ocean Sea [the Atlantic Ocean] to the said King and Queen and to their successors . . . with everything that there is in ready to leave Castile for the New World. Little is known about Ponce's anti-Carib campaign, but during the second half of 1515 and the first half of 1516, he and his men probably conducted at least three campaigns to hunt down and "pacify" (in other words, kill or enslave) the Carib raiders, using Puerto Rico as their base of operations.

Aside from his New World crusade against the Caribs, Ponce's return voyage to Florida was also delayed by events

them, as is set forth in certain documents which were drawn up regarding this donation in the manner described, which you may see if you so desire.

In consequence, Their Highnesses are Kings and Lords of these islands and mainland by virtue of said donation. Certain other isles and almost all [the native peoples] to whom this summons has been read have accepted Their Highnesses as such Kings and Lords, and have served, and serve, them as their subjects as they should, and must do, with good will and without offering any resistance. . . . You are constrained and obliged to do the same as they.

Consequently . . . we beseech and demand that you . . . accept the Church and Superior Organization of the whole world and recognize the Supreme Pontiff, called the Pope, and that in his name, you acknowledge the King and Queen . . . as the lords and superior authorities of these islands and mainlands. . . .

If you do not do this, however, . . . we warn you that, with the aid of God, we will enter you land against you with force and will make war in every place and by every means we can and are able. . . .

Pope Leo X held power of the Catholic Church during the time of "El Requerimiento" (The Requirement), which required conquistadors to inform all native peoples they encountered that they were to accept the message of Christianity and to accept the pope as their spiritual leader. Anything but complete agreement was dubbed rejection and was answered with violence.

taking place in the Old World. In January 1516, Ponce's mentor King Ferdinand died, leaving the crown to his and Isabella's teenage grandson, Carlos I. In the autumn of 1516, worried that the titles and privileges awarded him by the late king might be in jeopardy, Ponce sailed back to the now officially united kingdom of Spain to meet with his new sovereign. Ponce stayed in Spain for the next year and a half until May 1518. While he was there, Devereux and Murga Sanz believe, Ponce married a young woman of Seville named Juana de Pineda. Fuson strongly disagrees with Devereux and Murga Sanz, arguing that although no official death date has ever been located for Ponce's first wife, Leonor, several of Leonor's children and grandchildren cited 1519 as the year of her death, meaning that Ponce could not have remarried while he was in Spain from 1516 to mid-1518.

After returning to Puerto Rico in May 1518, Ponce spent much of the next two and a half years getting his affairs in order in Puerto Rico and Hispaniola (where he still owned his plantation at Salvaleón) and organizing his second expedition to Florida, a time consuming undertaking. As was the case with his first voyage, Ponce was responsible for hiring and paying the crew and providing all the necessary supplies for the journey. This time around, since colonization was one of the voyage's principal goals, those supplies included a number of horses, cows, sheep, goats and pigs as well as a variety of agricultural tools and seeds. Ponce also devoted much time to recruiting a group of men and women interested in settling in the new Spanish territory of Florida.

Little information has come down to us regarding Ponce's second voyage to Florida. Three letters composed shortly before the voyage, two written by Ponce himself and one by his son-in-law Antonio de la Gama, constitute the only surviving primary sources for the expedition. In the first letter, addressed to an influential church official in Spain in early February 1521, Ponce wrote that he was taking two ships on his upcoming expedition and would include as many passengers as "I am able to carry." Ponce gave two objectives for his voyage in the letter: to explore the new territory and to found a colony there. In a second letter written on the same day to King Carlos, Ponce provides another goal for his voyage—to ascertain if Florida was actually an island, as he had assumed during his first voyage, or "is connected with the land [of Mexico] or with some other land." The last surviving letter regarding Ponce's second Florida voyage from his son-in-law Antonio de la Gama to King Carlos reports that Ponce was scheduled to depart Puerto Rico on February 20 "to settle the Florida Island, and to make discoveries in the neighboring regions."

When Juan Ponce and his small fleet left Puerto Rico for Florida on February 20, 1521, he probably carried about 100 people with him. Oviedo, one of the few sixteenth-century historians to write anything about the second expedition, claims that Ponce was accompanied by 200 crew members, colonists, soldiers, and priests, but Fuson thinks that this number is inflated given the modest size of the two sailing vessels that comprised Ponce's fleet and the large number of horses and other animals he took with him. Since, according to Fuson, half as many passengers as Oviedo mentions would still have made for two very crowded ships, Fuson believes that Ponce's expedition could not have possibly included more than 100 people.

Ponce's voyage from Puerto Rico to Florida probably took between two and three weeks, but could have taken longer depending on such variables as weather, wind, currents, mechanical problems, or stopovers. Where Ponce landed in Florida is a mystery, but most scholars assume that he returned to the same general area of the Gulf Coast near modern-day Fort Myers and Charlotte Harbor he had visited in 1513, arriving there sometime after mid-March. Anthony Devereux believes that Ponce chose to return to the Fort Myers/Charlotte Harbor area because he still hoped to get his hands on the gold reputedly possessed by the local Calusa cacique, Chief Carlos.

Wherever they may have landed, Fuson believes that Ponce and his group managed to live for at least four months in their new Florida settlement before being driven out by the "bellicose and ferocious" Calusa, as Oviedo describes the Gulf Coast's most powerful Indian group. Sometime in late June or early July 1521, a major battle took place between the Spaniards and a much larger force of Calusa in which a number of Spaniards were killed or wounded. Among the injured was Juan Ponce, "a courageous captain and at the front" throughout the entire confrontation, according to Oviedo. Gravely wounded by a Calusa arrow, Ponce ordered his men to take him to Cuba, the nearest Spanish colony, to receive medical treatment. After his recovery, he planned to return to Florida with a larger number of soldiers and colonists to finish his conquest of the new territory for Spain, Oviedo reports.

But Ponce never got a chance to complete his conquest of Florida. His wound became infected and sometime in July 1521 he died in Havana, Cuba. Assuming a birth date of 1474, he would have been 47 years old. Nearly 40 years after his death, Ponce's remains were transported from Havana to the Church of Saint Thomas Aquinas in San Juan, Puerto Rico. In 1909, they were moved to the Cathedral of San Juan, where they still rest in a marble tomb inscribed with the following epitaph:

> Juan Ponce de León . . . whose gallant deeds were evidence of his noble and pure lineage, soldier in Granada, captain in Española [Hispaniola], conqueror and governor of San Juan del Boriquén [Puerto Rico]. Discoverer and first governor of Florida: valiant military man, skillful leader, loyal subject. Honest administrator, loving father and industrious and consistent colonist. . . .

Over the next four decades following Ponce's fateful voyage of 1521, five Spanish expeditions and one French expedition

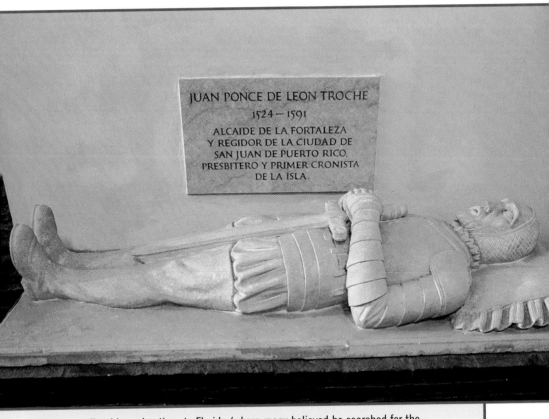

JUAN PONCE DE LEON TROCHE
1524 — 1591
ALCAIDE DE LA FORTALEZA
Y REGIDOR DE LA CIUDAD DE
SAN JUAN DE PUERTO RICO,
PRESBITERO Y PRIMER CRONISTA
DE LA ISLA.

After expanding his explorations to Florida (where many believed he searched for the fountain of youth), Ponce was injured in a battle with local Calusa tribesmen. Although not killed on the battlefield, his wound became infected and he later died in Havana, Cuba. His remains were eventually moved to San Juan, Puerto Rico, where this tomb commemorates his life.

visited Florida. In 1565, the first permanent European settlement and city in what would eventually become the continental United States was founded at St. Augustine in eastern Florida by the Spanish admiral, Pedro Menendez de Aviles.

As England's colonial empire in North America expanded during the seventeenth and eighteenth centuries, creeping ever farther down the Atlantic Coast, Spain's hold over Florida weakened. Nonetheless, with the exception of a 20-year period from 1763 to 1783 when Florida was under British control, Spain continued to rule most of the region until the second decade of the nineteenth century, when it was ceded to the United States in two units. Three centuries of Spanish hegemony in Florida, inaugurated when Juan Ponce de León boldly claimed the peninsula for King Ferdinand in 1513, had finally come to an end.

Chronology

c. 1474	Ponce is born in Santervás de Campos in the kingdom of Castile on the Iberian Peninsula.
c.1487–92	Ponce fights in the Reconquista to win Granada back from the Moors.
1492	The Reconquista ends when Granada surrenders to King Ferdinand and Queen Isabella; Columbus' first voyage to America.
1493	Ponce accompanies Christopher Columbus on his second expedition to the New World and sees the island of Puerto Rico for the first time.
1502	Ponce returns to Hispaniola with the new royally-appointed governor, Ovando.
1504	Ovando appoints Ponce frontier governor of Higüey in eastern Hispaniola.
1506–08	Ponce explores and conquers Puerto Rico and establishes the first Spanish settlement there at Caparra.
1509–11	Ponce serves as governor of Puerto Rico.
1511	Ponce loses his post as governor of Puerto Rico after Diego Columbus becomes viceroy of all the islands discovered by his late father.
1513	Ponce leads an expedition to the fabled island of Bimini but finds Florida and the Gulf Stream instead.
1514	In Spain, King Ferdinand appoints Ponce governor of Bimini/Florida and authorizes him to return to Florida to explore further and to found a colony.
1515–16	Ponce leads the fight to subdue the Carib Indians who had been raiding Spanish settlements in the Caribbean.

1516 Ponce returns to Spain to meet with the new king, Carlos I, and protect his privileges and rights.

1521 Ponce leads a second expedition to Florida to colonize the new territory in February.

Ponce dies in Havana, Cuba after being wounded in Florida by Calusa Indians in July.

Bibliography

Devereux, Anthony Q. *Juan Ponce de León, King Ferdinand and the Fountain of Youth.* Spartanburg, SC: The Reprint Company, 1993.

Dolan, Sean, *Juan Ponce de León.* New York: Chelsea House, 1995.

Fuentes, Carlos. *The Buried Mirror: Reflections on Spain and the New World.* Boston: Houghton Mifflin, 1992.

Fuson, Robert H. *Juan Ponce de León and the Spanish Discovery of Puerto Rico and Florida.* Blacksburg, VA: McDonald & Woodward, 2000.

Fuson, Robert H. *Legendary Islands of the Ocean Sea.* Sarasota, FL: Pineapple Press, 1995.

Gannon, Michael V. *The Cross in the Sand: The Early Catholic Church in Florida, 1513-1870.* Gainesville: University Presses of Florida, 1965.

Humble, Richard and the Editors of Time-Life Books. *The Explorers.* Alexandria, VA: Time-Life Books, 1978.

Morison, Samuel Eliot, *The European Discovery of America: The Southern Voyages, A.D. 1492-1616.* New York: Oxford University Press, 1974.

Murga Sanz, Vicente. "Florida," in Jose Agustin Balseiro, ed., *The Hispanic Presence in Florida: Yesterday and Today, 1513-1976.* Miami: E. A. Seemann, 1976.

Phillips, William D. and Carla Rahn Phillips. *The Worlds of Christopher Columbus.* Cambridge, UK: Cambridge University Press, 1992.

Sanderlin, George, ed. *Witness: Writings of Bartolomé de las Casas.* Maryknoll, NY: Orbis Books, 1992.

Shofner, Jerrell, *A Pictorial History of Florida.* Sarasota, FL: Pineapple Press, 1990.

Weddle, Robert S. *Spanish Sea: The Gulf of Mexico in North American Discovery, 1500-1685.* College Station: Texas A&M University Press, 1985.

Web Sources

The Conquest of Higuey
http://www.indiana.edu/~r317doc/dr/higuey/higuey3.html

The Taino World
http://www.elmuseo.org/taino/tainoworld.html

Encarta Online, S. V. "Christopher Columbus," "Ponce de León," and "Spain"
http://encarta.msn.com

Websites

The Catholic Encyclopedia: "Juan Ponce de Leon"
http://www.newadvent.org/Cathen/12228a.htm

Enchanted Learner: "Juan Ponce de Leon: Explorer"
http://www.enchantedlearning.com/explorers/page/d/deleon.shtml

The Floridians
http://www.floridahistory.org/floridians/textpg.htm

The Taino World
http://www.elmuseo.org/taino/tainoworld.html

Further Reading

Devereux, Anthony Q. *Juan Ponce de León, King Ferdinand, and the Fountain of Youth*. Spartanburg, SC: Reprint Company, 1993.

Dolan, Sean, *Juan Ponce de León*. New York: Chelsea House, 1995.

Dor-Ner, Zvi. *Columbus and the Age of Discovery*. New York: William Morrow, 1991.

Fuson, Robert H. *Juan Ponce de León and the Spanish Discovery of Puerto Rico and Florida*. Blacksburg, VA: McDonald & Woodward, 2000.

Morison, Samuel Eliot. *The European Discovery of America: The Southern Voyages, A.D. 1492-1616*. New York: Oxford University Press, 1974.

Murga Sanz, Vicente, "Florida," in Jose Agustin Balseiro, ed. *The Hispanic Presence in Florida: Yesterday and Today, 1513-1976*. Miami: E. A. Seemann, 1976.

Phillips, William D. and Carla Rahn Phillips. *The Worlds of Christopher Columbus*. Cambridge, UK: Cambridge University Press, 1992.

Shofner, Jerrell. *Florida Portrait: A Pictorial History of Florida*. Sarasota, FL: Pineapple Press, 1990.

Index

Picture Credits

About the Author

Louise Chipley Slavicek holds a master's degree in history from the University of Connecticut. She has written many articles on historical topics for young people's magazines and is the author of four other books for junior and senior high school students: *Life Among the Puritans*, *Confucianism*, *Women of the American Revolution*, and *Israel*. She lives in Ohio with her husband Jim, a research biologist, and their two children, Krista and Nathan.